What
AUGUSTINE
Says

What AUGUSTINE Says

Norman L. Geisler, Editor

Baker Book House
Grand Rapids, Michigan 49506

ISBN: 0-8010-0815-4

Library of Congress
Catalog Card Number: 82-72965

Printed in the United States of America

"Of True Religion" from *Augustine: Earlier Writings,* edited by John H. S. Burleigh
(volume VI: The Library of Christian Classics). Published simultaneously in Great
Britain and the U.S.A. by the S.C.M. Press, Ltd., London, and The Westminster Press,
Philadelphia. First published MCMLIII. Used by permission.

*To the many graduate students
with whom I have shared
in the wisdom
of Augustine.*

Contents

9 Ethics 201

Preface

Saint Augustine was one of the greatest Christian thinkers of all time. It is amazing that almost sixteen centuries later he is still one of the most quoted of all Christian writers. Yet most Christians do not have ready access to the approximately twenty volumes of his writings as found in *The Fathers of the Church*. Nor will many ever read the nearly five thousand pages translated in *The Nicene and Post-Nicene Fathers*.

What is more, Augustine did not write systematically on topics like God, man, sin, faith, reason, evil, ethics, and salvation. His great insights are scattered throughout thousands of pages in dozens of books. Having researched these topics throughout Augustine's writings, I am convinced that Augustine can contribute significantly to contemporary evangelical thinking.

To make Augustine's thoughts readily available, we have arranged them systematically. Their richness can only be fully appreciated in their fuller context. The more earnest student will want to use the references cited for this purpose.

We have found Augustine particularly helpful in the current evangelical discussions on apologetics, the inspiration of Scripture, the nature of God, the problem of evil, and ethics. Like any fallible teacher, Augustine sometimes erred. But as one sage wisely noted, we occasionally learn more from the errors of great minds than from the truths of lesser minds.

I wish to thank Scott Baker for his valuable assistance in the preparation of this manuscript.

Sources and Abbreviations

Unless otherwise designated all quotations are from A Select Library of the Nicene and Post-Nicene Fathers of the Christian Church, ed. Philip Schaff, first series, vols. 1–7 (1886–1888; reprint ed., Grand Rapids: Eerdmans, 1979).

Other quotations are designated as follows:

AS   An Augustine Synthesis, ed. Erich Przywara (1936; reprint ed., Gloucester, Mass.: Peter Smith, 1970).

FOC   The Writings of Saint Augustine, in Fathers of the Church, ed. Ludwig Schopp et al., vols. 1–19 (New York: CIMA, 1948–1954).

TR   "Of True Religion," trans. J. H. S. Burleigh (Philadelphia: Westminster, 1953).

1

Faith and Reason

I. Reason initially precedes faith.

A. Reason helps one judge whether authority is credible.

1. For who cannot see that thinking is prior to believing? For no one believes anything unless he has first thought that it is to be believed. . . . Although even belief itself is nothing else than to think [reason] with assent. *On the Predestination of the Saints* 5.

2. For my part, I should not believe the gospel except as moved by the authority of the Catholic Church. So when those on whose authority I have consented to believe in the gospel tell me not to believe in Manichaeus, how can I but consent? . . . : do you think me such a fool as to believe or not to believe as you like or dislike, without any reason? . . . Wherefore, if no clear proof of the apostleship of Manichaeus is found in the gospel, I will believe the Catholics rather than you. *Against the Epistle of Manichaeus* 5.

3. Again, if you say, You were right in believing the Catholics when they praised the gospel, but wrong in believing their vituperation of Manichaeus: do you think me such a fool as to believe or not to believe as you like or dislike, without any reason? It is therefore fairer and safer by far for me, having in one instance put faith in the Catholics, not to go over to you, till, instead of bidding me believe, you make me understand something in the clearest and most open manner. *Against the Epistle of Manichaeus* 5.

4. Authority demands belief and prepares man for reason. Reason leads to understanding and knowledge. But reason is not entirely absent from authority, for we have got to consider whom we have to believe, and the highest authority belongs to truth when it is clearly known. *Of True Religion* 24. TR

5. No one indeed believes anything, unless he has first thought that it is to be believed. For however suddenly, however rapidly, some thoughts fly before the will to believe . . . it is yet necessary that everything which is believed should be believed after thought has led the way; although belief itself is nothing other than to think with assent. . . . Every one who believes, thinks—both thinks in believing, and believes in thinking. *On the Predestination of the Saints* 5.

B. Reason precedes faith in reality, not in time.

6. In point of time, authority is first; but in the order of reality, reason is prior. *Divine Providence and the Problem of Evil* 2.9. FOC

7. [Faith] has priority by the order, not of nature or its inherent excellence, but of time. *Of True Religion* 24. TR

C. Reason tells us that it is reasonable to believe what we cannot ascertain by reason.

8. God forbid that He should hate in us that faculty by which He made us superior to all other living beings. Therefore, we must refuse so to believe as not to receive or seek a reason for our belief, since we could not believe at all if we did not have rational souls. So, then, in some points that bear on the doctrine of salvation, which we are not yet able to grasp by reason—but we shall be able to sometime—let faith precede reason, and let the heart be cleansed by faith so as to receive and bear the great light of reason; this is indeed reasonable. Therefore the Prophet said with reason: "If you will not believe, you will not understand"; thereby he undoubtedly made a distinction between these two things and advised us to believe first so as to be able to understand whatever we believe. *Letters* 120.1. FOC

D. Reason helps us understand the contents of what is to be believed.

9. For since "faith cometh by hearing; and hearing by the word of Christ" (Rom. x, 17), how can anyone believe him who preaches the faith if he (to say nothing of other points) does not understand the very tongue which he speaks? But unless, on the other hand, there were some things which we cannot understand unless we first believe them, the prophet would not say, "If you will not believe, you shall not understand" (Is. vii, 9. *sec.* LXX). Our understanding therefore contributes to the comprehension of that which it believes, and faith contributes to the belief of that which it comprehends. And the mind itself, in proportion as these things are more and more understood, profits in the very comprehension of them. AS, p. 59.

E. Reason helps us to believe what we cannot see.

10. The mysteries and secrets of the Kingdom of God first seek out believing men, that they may make them understand. For faith is understanding's step, and understanding is faith's reward. . . . To be sure thou dost see somewhat that thou mayest believe somewhat, and from that thou seest mayest believe what thou seest not. . . . God hath given thee eyes in the body, reason in the heart. Arouse the reason of the heart, awaken the interior inhabitant of thy interior eyes, let it take to its windows, let it examine God's Creation. . . . Believe on Him whom thou seest not because of those things which thou seest. *Sermons on New Testament Lessons* 126.1,3.

F. Reason removes objections to belief.

11. I have answered to the best of my power the questions proposed; but let him who proposed them become now a Christian at once, lest, if he delay until he has finished the discussion of all difficulties connected with the sacred books, he come to the end of this life before he pass from death to life. For it is reasonable that he inquire as to the resurrection of the dead before he is admitted to the Christian sacraments. Perhaps he ought also to be allowed to insist on preliminary discussion of the question proposed concerning Christ—why He came so late in the world's history, and of a few great questions besides, to which all others are subordinate. *Letters* 102.38.

G. Reason persuaded by evidence can call one to faith.

12. These topics are elsewhere more amply discussed, and in fundamental questions of doctrine every intricate point has been opened up by thorough investigation and debate; but faith gives the understanding access to these things, unbelief closes the door. What man might not be moved to faith in the doctrine of Christ by such a remarkable chain of events from the beginning, and by the manner in which the epochs of the world are linked together, so that our faith in regard to present things is assisted by what happened in the past, and the record of earlier and ancient things is attested by later and more recent events? *Letters* 137.4.

II. Faith precedes full understanding.

A. Faith logically precedes understanding.

13. But unless, on the other hand, there were some things which we cannot understand unless we first believe them, the prophet would not say, "If you will not believe, you shall not understand" (Is. vii, 9. *sec.* LXX). AS, p. 59.

14. We believe that we might know; for if we wished to know and then believe, we should not be able either to know or believe. *On the Gospel of John* 27.9.

15. First believe, then understand. *On the Creed* 4.

16. For there are innumerable questions the solution of which is not to be demanded before we believe, lest life be finished by us in unbelief. When, however, the Christian faith has been thoroughly received, these questions behove to be studied with the utmost diligence for the pious satisfaction of the minds of believers. Whatever is discovered by such study ought to be imparted to others without vain self-complacency; if anything still remains hidden, we must bear with patience an imperfection of knowledge which is not prejudicial to salvation. *Letters* 102.38.

> 1. It is reasonable to believe in what reason
>   by itself cannot understand.

17. Thus if an unbeliever asks of me the reason of my faith and hope, believing, I will give him this reason by which he may possibly understand, namely, how preposterous it is to demand before believing the reason of those things which he cannot understand. *Letters* 120.1.

> 2. It is reasonable for believers to ask reasons
>   about what they believe.

18. But if a believer asks a reason, that he may understand what he believes, his measure of intelligence must be considered and a reason given within the limits of his comprehension, so that he may add to his faith as much understanding as he is capable of, seeing to it however that in attaining to the plenitude and completion of knowledge he does not depart from the way of the faith. *Letters* 120.1.

B. Faith logically proceeds toward understanding.

19. Thus much I believed, at one time more strongly than another, yet did I ever believe both that Thou wert, and hadst a care of us, although I was ignorant both what was to be thought of Thy substance, and what way led, or led back to Thee. Seeing, then, that we were too weak by unaided reason to find out the truth, and for this cause needed the authority of the holy writings, I had now begun to believe that Thou wouldest by no means have given such excellency of authority to those Scriptures throughout all lands, had it not been Thy will thereby to be believed in, and thereby sought. For now those things which heretofore appeared incongruous to me in the Scripture, and used to offend me, having heard divers of them expounded reasonably, I referred to the depth of the mysteries, and its authority seemed to me all the more venerable and worthy of religious belief, in that, while it was visible for all to read it, it reserved the majesty of its secret within its profound significance, stooping to all in the great plainness of its language and lowliness of its style, yet exercising the application of such as are not light of heart. . . . *Confessions* 6.5.

20. Thou shouldst not therefore see in order that thou mayest believe, but believe in order that thou mayest see: believe so long as thou dost not see, let thou blush with shame when thou dost see. Let us therefore believe while the time of faith lasts, until the time of seeing comes. . . . We walk by faith, so long as we believe that which we do not see, but sight will be ours, when we see Him face to face, as He really is. *Sermons on New Testament Lessons* 38.2.

III. Faith rewards reason with clear understanding.

A. *Faith overcomes deception, the result of sin.*

21. Falsehood arises not because things deceive us, for they can show the beholder nothing but their form. . . . It is sin which deceives the soul, when they seek something that is true but abandon or neglect truth. They love the works of the artificer more than the artificer of his art. . . . God is not offered to the corporeal senses, and transcends even the mind. *Of True Religion* 36. TR

22. In the order of nature it holds that when we learn anything, authority precedes reasoning. For a reason may seem weak when, after it is given, it claims authority to support it. But because the minds of men are obscured by familiarity with darkness, which covers them in a night of sins and evil habits, and cannot perceive in a way proper to the clarity and purity of reason, there is most wholesome provision for bringing the faltering eye into the light of truth under the kindly shade of authority. But since we have to do with those who are unordered in all their thoughts and words and actions, and who are bent on nothing more than on beginning with argument, I will, as a concession to them, take what I think to be a wrong method in disputation. For it delights me to imitate, as far as I can, the gentleness of my Lord Jesus Christ, who took on Himself the evil death itself, wishing to free us from it. *On the Morals of the Catholic Church* 2.

23. The sin which they committed was so great that it impaired all human nature—in this sense, that the nature has been transmitted to posterity with a propensity to sin and a necessity to die. *City of God* 14.1.

B. Only faith can overcome deception.

24. Again, before we have the power to conceive and perceive God, as he can be conceived and perceived—for this is permitted to the clean of heart, since, "Blessed are the clean of heart: for they shall see God" (Matt. v, 8)—unless He be loved by faith, it will not be possible for the heart to be cleansed so that it may be apt and meet to see Him. For where are those three things, for the building up of which in the mind the whole apparatus of the divine Scriptures has been erected, namely faith, hope, and charity (I Cor. xiii, 13), except in a mind believing what it does not yet see, and hoping and loving what it believes? He therefore who is not known, but yet is believed, can be loved. . . . Faith, therefore, avails to the knowledge and to the love of God, not as though of one wholly unknown or not loved at all, but to the end that He may be known more clearly and loved more steadfastly. *On the Trinity* 8.4,9.

25. Nor does anyone become fit to discover God unless he shall have first believed what he is later to come to know. *On Free Will* 2.6.

26. Faith seeks, understanding finds; whence the prophet saith, "If you shall not have believed, you shall not understand." *On the Trinity* 15.2.

IV. Reason is adequate to demonstrate God's existence.

A. The existence of God can be proven by reason.

27. But, why did it please the eternal God to create heaven and earth at that special time, seeing that He had not done so earlier? If the purpose of those who pose this question is to protest that the world is eternal, without beginning, and, therefore, not created by God, then they are far from the truth and are raving with the deadly disease of irreligion. For, quite apart from the voice of the Prophets, the very order, changes, and movements in the universe, the very beauty of form in all that is visible, proclaim, however silently, both that the world was created and also that its Creator could be none other than God whose greatness and beauty are both ineffable and invisible. *City of God* 11.4.

1. The cosmological argument

28. Behold, the heavens and the earth are; they proclaim that they were created; for they change and vary. Whereas whatsoever hath not been made, and yet is, hath nothing in it, which before it had not; and this it is, to change and vary. They proclaim also, that they made not themselves; "therefore we are, because we have been made; we were not therefore, before we were, so as to make ourselves." Now the evidence of the thing, is the voice of the speakers. Thou therefore, Lord, madest them; who art beautiful, for they are beautiful; who art good, for they are good; who art, for they are; yet are they not beautiful nor good, nor are they, as Thou their Creator art; compared with Whom, they are neither beautiful, nor good, nor are. This we know, thanks be to Thee. And our knowledge, compared with Thy knowledge, is ignorance. *Confessions* 11.4.

29. And thus, by degrees, I passed from bodies to the soul, which makes use of the senses of the body to perceive; and thence to its inward faculty, to which the bodily senses represent outward things, and up to which reach the capabilities of beasts; and thence, again, I passed on to the reasoning faculty, unto which whatever is received from the senses of the body is referred to be judged, which also, finding itself to be variable in me, raised itself up to its own intelligence, and from habit drew away my thoughts, withdrawing itself from the crowds of contradictory phantasms; that so it might find out that light by which it was besprinkled, when, without all doubting, it cried out, that the unchangeable was to be preferred before the changeable; whence also it knew that unchangeable, which, unless it had in some way known, it could have had no sure ground for preferring it to the changeable. And thus, with the flash of a trembling glance, it arrived at that which is. And then I saw Thy invisible things understood by the things that are made. *Confessions* 7.17.

2. The proof from perfection

30. There is an "eternal immutable Form which is neither extended nor varied in time, and through which all mutable things can receive a form and according to their kind fulfill and accomplish their ordered rhythms in space and time." *On Free Will* 2.44.

3. The implied ontological argument

31. For I was so struggling to find out the rest, as having already found that what was incorruptible must be better than the corruptible; and Thee, therefore, whatsoever Thou wert, did I acknowledge to be incorruptible. For never yet was, nor will be, a soul able to conceive of anything better than Thou, who art the highest and best good. *Confessions* 7.4.

4. The teleological argument

32. But how didst Thou make the heaven and the earth? and what the engine of Thy so mighty fabric? For it was not as a human artificer, forming one body from another, according to the discretion of his mind, which can in some way invest with such a form, as it seeth in itself by its inward eye. And whence should he be able to do this, unless Thou hadst made that mind? and he invests with a form what already existeth, and hath a being, as clay, or stone, or wood, or gold, or the like. And whence should they be, hadst not Thou appointed them? Thou madest the artificer his body, Thou the mind commanding the limbs, Thou the matter whereof he makes any thing; Thou the apprehension whereby to take in his art, and see within what he doth without; Thou the sense of his body, whereby, as by an interpreter, he may from mind to matter, convey that which he doth, and report to his mind what is done; that it within may consult the truth, which presideth over itself, whether it be well done or no. All these praise Thee, the Creator of all. *Confessions* 11.5.

33. In His providence He has given to ants and to bees senses superior to those given to asses and camels; He creates the huge proportions of the fig-tree from one of the minutest of seeds, although many smaller plants spring from much larger seeds; He has endowed the small pupil of the eye with a power which by one glance sweeps almost half the sky in a moment. . . . But in all the varied movements of the creature what work of God's is not wonderful? And yet these daily wonders have by familiarity become small in our esteem. Nay, how many common objects are trodden underfoot which, if carefully examined, amaze us! *Letters* 137.2,3.

5. The argument from truth

34. *Augustine:* But suppose we could find something which you are certain not only exists but is also superior to our reason, would you hesitate to call this reality, whatever it is, God? . . . For God Himself has given this reason of yours the power to think of Him with such reverence and truth. But I will ask you this: if you should find that there is nothing above our reason but an eternal and changeless reality, would you hesitate to say that this is God? You notice how bodies are subject to change, and is clear that the living principle animating the body is not free from change but passes through various states. And reason itself is clearly shown to be changeable, seeing that at one time it endeavors to reach the truth, and at another time it does not, sometimes it arrives at the truth, sometimes it does not. If reason sees something eternal and changeless not by any bodily organ, neither by touch nor taste nor smell nor hearing nor sight, nor by any sense inferior to it, but sees this of itself, and sees at the same time its own inferiority, it will have to acknowledge that this being is its God.

Evodius: I will openly acknowledge that to be God, if, as all agree, there is nothing higher existing.

Augustine: Good! It will be enough for me to show that something of this kind exists. Either you will admit that *this* is God or, if there is something higher, you will admit that *it* is God. Accordingly, whether there exists something higher or not, it will become clear that God exists, when, with His assistance, I shall prove, as I promised, that there exists something above reason. *On Free Will* 2.6. FOC

B. All truth is God's truth.

35. Moreover, if those who are called philosophers, and especially the Platonists, have said aught that is true and in harmony with our faith, we are not only not to shrink from it, but to claim it for our own use from those who have unlawful possession of it . . . in the same way all branches of heathen learning have not only false and superstitious fancies and heavy burdens of unnecessary toil, which every one of us, when going out under the leadership of Christ from the fellowship of the heathen, ought to abhor and avoid; but they contain also liberal instruction which is better adapted to the use of the truth, and some most excellent precepts of morality; and some truths in regard even to the worship of the One God are found among them. Now these are, so to speak, their gold and silver, which they did not create themselves, but dug out of the mines of God's providence which are everywhere scattered abroad, and are perversely and unlawfully prostituting to the worship of devils. These, therefore, the Christian, when he separates himself in spirit from the miserable fellowship of these men, ought to take away from them, and to devote to their proper use in preaching the gospel. *On Christian Doctrine* 2.40.

C. Plato would be a Christian today.

36. If Plato and the rest of them, in whose names men glory, were to come to life again and find the churches full and the temples empty, . . . they would perhaps say . . . : That is what we did not dare to preach to the people. . . . So if these men [Plato, et al.] could live their lives again today, they would see by whose authority measures are best taken for man's salvation, and, with the change of a few words and sentiments, they would become Christians, as many Platonists of recent times have done. *Of True Religion* 4. TR

37. However philosophers may boast, anyone can easily understand that religion is not to be sought from them. For they take part in the religious rites of their fellow-citizens, but in their schools teach divergent and contrary opinions about the nature of their gods and of the chief good, as the multitude can testify. If we could see this one great vice healed by the Christian discipline, no one should deny that that would be an achievement worthy of all possible praise. *Of True Religion* 4. TR

D. Reason is inherently more excellent than faith.

38. In so far as concerns the nature of man, there is in him nothing better than the mind and reason. But he who would live blessedly ought not to live according to them; for then he would live according to man, whereas he ought to live according to God, so that he may attain to blessedness. And to accomplish this, our mind must not be content with itself, but must be subjected to God. *Retractations* 1.1.

V. Reason confirms faith with evidence.

A. Faith is confirmed through historical miracles.

1. Miracles are great evidence.

39. He was to do also some things peculiar to Himself, namely, to be born of a virgin, to rise from the dead, to ascend to heaven. I know not what greater things he can look for who thinks these too little for God to do. *Letters* 137.4.

40. "But," they say, "the proofs of so great majesty did not shine forth with adequate fulness of evidence; for the casting out of devils, the healing of the sick, and the restoration of the dead to life are but small works for God to do, if the others who have wrought similar wonders be borne in mind." We ourselves admit that the prophets wrought some miracles like those performed by Christ. For among these miracles what is more wonderful than the raising of the dead? *Letters* 137.4.

41. If, however, the objection to believing this miracle is, that it happened only once, ask the friend who is still perplexed by this, whether instances may not be quoted from secular literature of events which were, like this one, unique, and which, nevertheless, are believed, not merely as fables are believed by the simple, but with that faith with which the history of facts is received—ask him, I beseech you, this question. *Letters* 143.12.

42. Therefore God, who made the visible heaven and earth, does not disdain to work visible miracles in heaven or earth, that He may thereby awaken the soul which is immersed in things visible to worship Himself, the Invisible. But the place and time of these miracles are dependent on His unchangeable will, in which things future are ordered as if already they were accomplished. *City of God* 10.12.

2. Miracles confirm God's promises to Israel.

43. I should seem tedious were I to recount all ancient miracles, which were wrought in attestation of God's promises which He made to Abraham thousands of years ago, that in his seed all the nations of the earth should be blessed. *City of God* 10.8.

3. Miracles strengthen faith of believers.

44. The belief of the resurrection of our Lord from the dead, and His ascension into heaven, has strengthened our faith by adding a great buttress of hope. *On Christian Doctrine* 1.15.

4. Miracles help produce faith.

45. He restored to the blind those eyes which death was sure some time to close; He raised Lazarus from the dead, who was to die again. And whatever He did for the health of bodies, He did it not to the end that they should exist for evermore; whereas at the last He will give eternal health even to the body itself. But because those things which were not seen were not believed, by means of those temporal things which were seen He built up faith in those things which were not seen. Let no one therefore say that our Lord Jesus Christ doeth not those things now, and on this account prefer the former to the present ages of the Church. . . . The Lord did those things to invite us to the faith. *Sermons on New Testament Lessons* 88.1–3.

46. Why, they say, are those miracles, which you affirm were wrought formerly, wrought no longer? I might, indeed, reply that miracles were necessary before the world believed, in order that it might believe. And whoever now-a-days demands to see prodigies that he may believe, is himself a great prodigy, because he does not believe, though the whole world does. But they make these objections. . . . *City of God* 22.8.

5. There is strong evidence for the resurrection of Christ.

47. Wherefore, since it was not necessary that He should make a new world, He made new things in the world. For that a man should be born of a virgin, and raised from the dead to eternal life, and exalted above the heavens, is perchance a work involving a greater exertion of power than the creating of a world. Here, probably, objectors may answer that they do not believe that these things took place. What, then, can be done for men who despise smaller evidences as inadequate, and reject greater evidences as incredible? That life has been restored to the dead is believed, because it has been accomplished by others, and is too small a work to prove him who performs it to be God: that a true body was created in a virgin, and being raised from death to eternal life, was taken up to heaven, is not believed, because no one else has done this, and it is what God alone could do. On this principle every man is to accept with equanimity whatever he thinks easy for himself not indeed to do, but to conceive, and is to reject as false and fictitious whatever goes beyond that limit. I beseech you, do not be like these men. *Letters* 137.4.

48. It is indubitable that the resurrection of Christ, and His ascension into heaven with the flesh in which He rose, is already preached and believed in the whole world. If it is not credible, how is it that it has already received credence in the whole world? If a number of noble, exalted, and learned men had said that they had witnessed it, and had been at pains to publish what they had witnessed, it were not wonderful that the world should have believed it, but it were very stubborn to refuse credence; but if, as is true, the world has believed a few obscure, inconsiderable, uneducated persons, who state and write that they witnessed it, is it not unreasonable that a handful of wrong headed men should oppose themselves to the creed of the whole world, and refuse their belief? . . . That the one incredibility of the resurrection and ascension of Jesus Christ may be believed, we accumulate the testimonies of countless incredible miracles, but even so we do not bend the frightful obstinacy of these sceptics. But if they do not believe that these miracles were wrought by Christ's apostles to gain credence to their preaching of His resurrection and ascension, this one grand miracle suffices for us, that the whole world has believed without any miracles. *City of God* 22.5.

49. Would the human mind have refused to listen to or believe in the resurrection of Christ's body and its ascension into heaven, and have scouted it as an impossibility, had not the divinity of the truth itself, or the truth of the divinity, and corroborating miraculous signs, proved that it could happen and had happened? . . . But we cannot deny that many miracles were wrought to confirm that one grand and health-giving miracle of Christ's ascension to heaven with the flesh in which He rose. For these most trustworthy books of ours contain in one narrative both the miracles that were wrought and the creed which they were wrought to confirm. The miracles were published that they might produce faith, and the faith which they produced brought them into greater prominence. *City of God* 22.7.

B. Faith is confirmed through fulfilled prophecy.

50. But there were other truly important and divine events which they predicted, in so far as it was given them to know the will of God. For the incarnation of Christ, and all those important marvels that were accomplished in Him, and done in His name; the repentance of men and the conversion of their wills to God; the remission of sins, the grace of righteousness, the faith of the pious, and the multitudes in all parts of the world who believe in the true divinity; the overthrow of idolatry and demon worship, and the testing of the faithful by trials; the purification of those who persevered, and their deliverance from all evil; the day of judgment, the resurrection of the dead, the eternal damnation of the community of the ungodly, and the eternal kingdom of the most glorious city of God, ever-blessed in the enjoyment of the vision of God,—these things were predicted and promised in the Scriptures of this way; and of these we see so many fulfilled, that we justly and piously trust that the rest will also come to pass. *City of God* 10.32.

51. But they are not deceived, who think that we believe in Christ without any proofs concerning Christs. For what are clearer proofs than those things, which we now see to have been foretold and fulfilled. *Letters* 138.15.

52. All these things are now seen to be accomplished, in exact fulfilment of the predictions which we read in Scripture; and from these important and numerous instances of fulfilled prophecy, the fulfilment of the predictions which remain is confidently expected. Where, then, is the mind, having aspirations after eternity, and moved by the shortness of this present life, which can resist the clearness and perfection of these evidences of the divine origin of our faith? *Letters* 137.4.

C. Faith is confirmed through the conversion of pagans.

53. Even if there were no preceding testimonies concerning Christ and the Church, who is there whom the sudden shining of the divine brightness on the human race ought not to move to belief; when we see the false gods abandoned, their images everywhere shattered, their temples overthrown or converted to other uses, the many vain rites plucked out by the roots from the most inveterate usage of men, and the one true God invoked by all? And this has been brought about by one Man, who by men was mocked, seized, bound, scourged, smitten with the palm of the hand, reviled, crucified, and put to death. *On Faith of Things Unseen* 7.10. FOC

D. Faith is confirmed through the nature of the Bible.

54. Consider, moreover, the style in which Sacred Scripture is composed,—how accessible it is to all men, though its deeper mysteries are penetrable to very few. The plain truths which it contains it declares in the artless language of familiar friendship to the hearts both of the unlearned and of the learned. . . . *Letters* 137.4.

VI. Faith is more profound than reason.

A. Faith and reason are distinguishable.

55. We can know by our own witness things which are presented to our senses, either interior or exterior. In fact, we say a thing is "present" because it is "presented" to our senses. For example, anything before our very eyes is said to be present. But, when things are not present to our senses, we cannot know them on our own authority. So we seek out and believe witnesses to whose senses, we believe, these things are or were present. *City of God* 11.3.

56. What then we understand, we owe to reason; what we believe, to authority; what we have an opinion on, to error. *On the Profit of Believing* 25.

57. Hold fast whatever truth you have been able to grasp, and attribute it to the Catholic Church. Reject what is false. . . . What is doubtful believe until either reason teaches or authority lays down that it is to be rejected or that it is true, or that it has to be believed always. *Of True Religion* 10. TR

B. Faith transcends reason.

58. Of all visible things, the universe is the greatest; of all invisible realities, the greatest is God. That the world exists we can see; we believe in the existence of God. But there is no one we can more safely trust than God Himself in regard to the fact that it was He who made the world. Where has He told us so? Nowhere more distinctly than in the Holy Scriptures where His Prophet said: "In the beginning God created the heavens and the earth." Well, but was the Prophet present when God made heaven and earth? No; but the Wisdom of God by whom all things were made was there. And this Wisdom, entering into holy souls, makes of them the friends and prophets of God and reveals to them, silently and interiorly, what God has done. *City of God* 11.4.

59. We cannot understand God unless we understand something. By faith we understand more. AS, p. 59.

60. Therefore, what I understand I also believe, but I do not understand everything that I believe; for all which I understand I know, but I do not know all that I believe. But still I am not unmindful of the utility of believing many things which are not known. . . . And though the majority of things must remain unknown to me, yet I do know what is the utility of believing. *Concerning the Teacher* 11.

VII. Faith and reason complement each other.

A. Faith and reason are separate sources of truth.

61. I have written these things in order to show that whoever is disposed to maintain and vindicate any one of these four theories of the soul's origin, must bring forward, either from the Scriptures received into ecclesiastical authority, passages which do not admit of any other interpretation,—as the statement that God made man,— or reasonings founded on premises so obviously true that to call them in question would be madness, such as the statement that none but the living are capable of knowledge or of error; for a statement like this does not require the authority of Scripture to prove its truth, as if the common sense of mankind did not of itself announce its truth with such transparent cogency of reason, that whoever contradicts it must be held to be hopelessly mad. *Letters* 143.11.

62. The explanation, then, of the goodness of creation is the goodness of God. It is a reasonable and sufficient explanation whether considered in the light of philosophy or of faith. It puts an end to all controversies concerning the origin of the world. *City of God* 11.22.

B. Faith and reason never contradict.

63. For if reason be found contradicting the authority of Divine Scriptures, it only deceives by a semblance of truth, however acute it be, for its deductions cannot in that case be true. On the other hand, if, against the most manifest and reliable testimony of reason, anything be set up claiming to have the authority of the Holy Scriptures, he who does this does it through a misapprehension of what he has read, and is setting up against the truth not the real meaning of Scripture, which he has failed to discover, but an opinion of his own; he alleges not what he has found in the Scriptures, but what he has found in himself as their interpreter. *Letters* 143.7.

64. The Christian heeds carefully the apostolic admonition which says: "See to it that no one deceives you by philosophy and vain deceit . . . according to the elements of the world." But the same Apostle [Paul] tells him not to decry all as materialistic philosophers, for of some he says: "What may be known about God is manifest to them. For God has manifested it to them. For since the creation of the world his invisible attributes are clearly seen—his everlasting power also and divinity—being understood through the things that are made." And again, speaking to the Athenians, after the magnificent remark about which so few can appreciate, namely, that "in Him we live and move and have our being," he went on to add: "as indeed some of your own (poets) have said." *City of God* 8.10.

VIII. Faith and reason can be used to show truth in an extraordinary manner.

A. *Heretics can awaken men to faith.*

65. So, many are awakened from sleep by the heretics, so that they may see God's light and be glad. *Of True Religion* 8. TR

B. *God can use angels or direct revelation to the heathen.*

66. Omnipotent God may himself show the truth, or he may use good angels or men to assist men of good will to behold and grasp the truth. *Of True Religion* 10. TR

2

The Bible

I. The inspiration of the Bible

A. Descriptions of the Bible

67. 1. Holy Scripture. *City of God* 15.8.

68. 2. Sacred Scripture. *City of God* 9.5.

69. 3. Divine Revelation. *City of God* 8.2.

70. 4. Oracles of God. *Expositions on the Book of Psalms* 137.7.

71. 5. Divine Scripture. *Enchiridion* 1.

72. 6. Words of God. *City of God* 10.1.

73. 7. God's Word. *Expositions on the Book of Psalms* 147.10.

74. 8. Divine Oracles. *Letters* 55.37.

75. 9. Infallible Scripture. *City of God* 11.6.

B. The source of the Bible

1. The Bible is inspired of God.

76. This Mediator, first through the Prophets, then by His own lips, afterwards through the Apostles, revealed whatever He considered necessary. He also inspired the Scripture, which is regarded as canonical and of supreme authority and to which we give credence concerning all those truths we ought to know and yet, of ourselves, are unable to learn. *City of God* 11.2.

2. The Bible is an oracle of the Holy Spirit.

77. What say ye to me, O ye objectors whom I was addressing, and who yet believe that Moses was the holy servant of God, and that his books were the oracles of the Holy Ghost? *Confessions* 12.15.

3. The Bible is the writing of the Holy Spirit.

78. Most eagerly, then, did I seize that venerable writing of Thy Spirit, but more especially the Apostle Paul; and those difficulties vanished away, in which he at one time appeared to me to contradict himself, and the text of his discourse not to agree with the testimonies of the Law and the Prophets. *Confessions* 7.21.

4. The Bible comes from the mouth of God.

79. "With my lips have I been telling of all the judgments of Thy mouth" (ver. 13); that is, I have kept silent nothing of Thy judgments, which Thou didst will should become known to me through Thy words, but I have been telling of all of them without exception with my lips. This he seemeth to me to signify, since he saith not, all Thy judgments, but, "all the judgments of Thy mouth;" that is, which Thou hast revealed unto me: that by His mouth we may understand His word, which He hath discovered unto us in many revelations of the Saints, and in the two Testaments; all which judgments the Church ceaseth not to declare at all times with her lips. *Expositions on the Book of Psalms* 119.12.

C. *The marks of inspiration*

1. The Bible has many names that indicate divine authorship (see 67–75).

2. Writers are inspired instruments.

80. And so, when the inspired writer states that God rested, his words are most appropriately interpreted to mean the rest of those who rest in God and of whose rest God is the cause. And the prophecy also promises to those to whom it speaks and for whom it was written that, if by faith they have drawn as close to God as is possible in this life, then, after doing the good works which God operates in and through them, they shall enjoy in Him eternal rest. *City of God* 11.8.

3. The Holy Writ is an inspired document.

a) The Bible is dictated by the Holy Spirit.

81. Therefore, when those disciples have written matters which He declared and spake to them, it ought not by any means to be said that He has written nothing Himself; since the truth is, that His members have accomplished only what they became acquainted with by the repeated [i.e., dictated, Lt. *dictis*] statements of the Head. For all that He was minded to give for our perusal on the subject of His own doings and sayings, He commanded to be written by those disciples, whom He thus used as if they were His own hands. *Harmony of the Gospels* 1.35.

b) Every jot and tittle comes from God.

82. So too we conceive of all that has been recorded by the inspiration of the Holy Ghost . . . [who] has placed, so to speak, the seeds of saving truth in each letter as far as possible. *Commentary on Psalms* 1.4.

c) The meaning of the words, not mere words, is important.

83. Consequently, when these translators, while not departing from the real mind of God from which these sayings proceeded, and to the expression of which the words ought to be subservient, gave a different form to some matters in their reproduction of the text, they had no intention of exemplifying anything else than the very thing which we now admiringly contemplate in that kind of harmonious diversity which marks the four evangelists, and in the light of which it is made clear that there is no failure from strict truth, although one historian may give an account of some theme in a manner different indeed from another, and yet not so different as to involve an actual departure from the sense intended by the person with whom he is bound to be in concord and agreement. . . . The fact rather is, that the theme itself which is to be expressed is so decidedly deemed of superior importance to the words in which it has to be expressed, that we would be under no obligation to ask about them at all, if it were possible for us to know the truth without the terms, as God knows it, and as His angels also know it in Him. *Harmony of the Gospels* 2.66.

84. Seeing, then, that the case stands thus, from these varied and yet not inconsistent modes of statement adopted by the evangelists, we evidently learn a lesson of the utmost utility, and of great necessity,—namely, that in any man's words the thing which we ought narrowly to regard is only the writer's thought which was meant to be expressed, and to which the words ought to be subservient; and further, that we should not suppose one to be giving an incorrect statement, if he happens to convey in different words what the person really meant whose words he fails to reproduce literally. And we ought not to let the wretched cavillers at words fancy that truth must be tied somehow or other to the jots and tittles of letters; whereas the fact is, that not in the matter of words only, but equally in all other methods by which sentiments are indicated, the sentiment itself, and nothing else, is what ought to be looked at. *Harmony of the Gospels* 2.28.

II. The authority of the Bible

A. *The Bible has supreme authority.*

85. This Mediator, first through the Prophets, then by His own lips, afterwards through the Apostles, revealed whatever He considered necessary. He also inspired the Scripture, which is regarded as canonical and of supreme authority and to which we give credence concerning all those truths we ought to know and yet, of ourselves, are unable to learn. *City of God* 11.3.

B. *The Bible has unique authority* (sola Scriptura).

86. However, if you inquire or recall to memory the opinion of our Ambrose, and also of our Cyprian, on the point in question, you will perhaps find that I have not been without some whose footsteps I follow in that which I have maintained. At the same time, as I have said already, it is to the canonical Scriptures alone that I am bound to yield such implicit subjection as to follow their teaching, without admitting the slightest suspicion that in them any mistake or any statement intended to mislead could find a place. *Letters* 82.3.

87. In the innumerable books that have been written latterly we may sometimes find the same truth as in Scripture, but there is not the same authority. Scripture has a sacredness peculiar to itself. . . . But in consequence of the sacred writing, we are bound to receive as true whatever the canon shows to have been said by even one prophet, or apostle, or evangelist. *Reply to Faustus the Manichaean* 11.5.

C. The Bible has authority over all other writings.

88. The expression, "City of God," which I have been using is justified by the Scripture whose divine authority puts it above the literature of all other people and brings under its sway every type of human genius—and that, not by some casual intellectual reaction, but by a disposition of Divine Providence. *City of God* 11.1.

89. In order to leave room for such profitable discussions of difficult questions, there is a distinct boundary line separating all productions subsequent to apostolic times from the authoritative canonical books of the Old and New Testaments. The authority of these books has come down to us from the apostles through the successions of bishops and the extension of the Church, and, from a position of lofty supremacy, claims the submission of every faithful and pious mind. *Reply to Faustus the Manichaean* 11.5.

90. All those Catholic expounders of the divine Scripture, both Old and New, whom I have been able to read, who have written before me concerning the Trinity . . . have purposed to teach . . . this doctrine, that the Father, Son, and the Holy Spirit intimate a divine unity of one and the same substance in an indivisible equality, and therefore that they are not three Gods, but one God. *On the Trinity* 1.4.

D. *The Bible is the canonical standard for all believers.*

91. This is most pertinent to the matter which I have in hand,— namely, the confirmation of the universal and unquestionable truth of the Divine Scriptures, which have been delivered to us for our edification in the faith, not by unknown men, but by the apostles, and have on this account been received as the authoritative canonical standard. *Letters* 82.2.

92. But in consequence of the distinctive peculiarity of the sacred writings, we are bound to receive as true whatever the canon shows to have been said by even one prophet, or apostle, or evangelist. Otherwise, not a single page will be left for the guidance of human fallibility. . . . *Reply to Faustus the Manichaean* 11.5.

93. On questions of this kind, however, I do not bestow much labour; because, even if the statement objected to does not admit of unanswerable vindication, it is mine only; it is not an utterance of that Author whose words it is impiety to reject, even when, through our misapprehension of their meaning, the interpretation which we put on them deserves to be rejected. *Letters* 143.2.

III. The inerrancy of the Bible

A. *The Bible does not contradict itself.*

　　1. Those who allege contradictions see only part
　　　of the evidence.

94. Those who allege contradictions in the Bible "examine only those testimonies of Scripture which support their peculiar view, regardless of the full and perfect meaning of such passages as exhibit the opposite side of the truth." *Commentary on Romans* 111.7.

　　2. There are obscurities but no contradictions.

95. "The Lord taketh up the gentle" (ver. 6). For example; thou understandest not, thou failest to understand, canst not attain: honour God's Scripture, honour God's Word, though it be not plain: in reverence wait for understanding. Be not wanton to accuse either the obscurity or seeming contradiction of Scripture. There is nothing in it contradictory: somewhat there is which is obscure, not in order that it may be denied thee, but that it may exercise him that shall afterward receive it. *Expositions on the Book of Psalms* 147.10.

96. Accordingly the Holy Spirit has, with admirable wisdom and care for our welfare, so arranged the Holy Scriptures as by the plainer passages to satisfy our hunger, and by the more obscure to stimulate our appetite. For almost nothing is dug out of those obscure passages which may not be found set forth in the plainest language elsewhere. *On Christian Doctrine* 2.6.

> 3. The Old and New Testaments do not contradict each other.

97. We must fear, lest the divine precepts should be contrary to one another. But no: let us understand that there is the most perfect agreement in them, let us not follow the conceits of certain vain ones, who in their error think that the two Testaments in the Old and New Books are contrary to each other; that so we should think that there is any contradiction here, because one is in the book of Solomon, and the other in the Gospel. For if any one unskilful in, and a reviler of the divine Scriptures, were to say, "See where the two Testaments contradict each other." *Sermons on New Testament Lessons* 32.8.

> 4. No part of the Bible contradicts any other part.

98. For the utterances of Scripture, harmonious as if from the mouth of one man, commend themselves to the belief of the most accurate and clear-sighted piety, and demand for their discovery and confirmation the calmest intelligence and the most ingenious research. *Reply to Faustus the Manichaean* 11.6.

> 5. The Bible has no more difficulties than nature.

99. Whoever has once received these Scriptures as inspired by the Creator of the world, must expect to find in them all the difficulties which meet those who investigate the system of the universe. *Commentary on Psalms* 1.4.

B. The Bible contains no errors.

1. It is impossible to have falsehood in the Bible.

100. I do not say this in order that you may recover the faculty of spiritual sight,—far be it from me to say that you have lost it!—but that, having eyes both clear and quick in discernment, you may turn them towards that from which, in unaccountable dissimulation, you have turned them away, refusing to see the calamitous consequences which would follow on our once admitting that a writer of the divine books could in any part of his work honourably and piously utter a falsehood. *Letters* 40.4.

2. Only the Bible must be inerrant.

101. As regards our writings, which are not a rule of faith or practice, but only a help to edification, we may suppose that they contain some things falling short of the truth in obscure and recondite matters, and that these mistakes may or may not be corrected in subsequent treatises. For we are of those of whom the apostle says: "And if ye be otherwise minded, God shall reveal even this unto you." Such writings are read with the right of judgment, and without any obligation to believe. *Reply to Faustus the Manichaean* 11.5.

3. All errors are due to copyists or translators.

102. For I confess to your Charity that I have learned to yield this respect and honour only to the canonical books of Scripture: of these alone do I most firmly believe that the authors were completely free from error. And if in these writings I am perplexed by anything which appears to me opposed to truth, I do not hesitate to suppose that either the manuscript is faulty, or the translator has not caught the meaning of what was said, or I myself have failed to understand it. As to all other writings, in reading them, however great the superiority of the authors to myself in sanctity and learning, I do not accept their teaching as true on the mere ground of the opinion being held by them; but only because they have succeeded in convincing my judgment of its truth either by means of these canonical writings themselves, or by arguments addressed to my reason. I believe, my brother, that this is your own opinion as well as mine. *Letters* 82.3.

103. If we are perplexed by an apparent contradiction in Scripture, it is not allowable to say, The author of this book is mistaken; but either the manuscript is faulty, or the translation is wrong, or you have not understood. *Reply to Faustus the Manichaean* 11.5.

   4. Even one error in the autograph would undermine
   the whole Bible.

104. For if you once admit into such a high sanctuary of authority one false statement as made in the way of duty, there will not be left a single sentence of those books which, if appearing to any one difficult in practice or hard to believe, may not by the same fatal rule be explained away, as a statement in which, intentionally, and under a sense of duty, the author declared what was not true. *Letters* 28.3.

105. For if it be the case that statements untrue in themselves, but made, as it were, out of a sense of duty in the interest of religion, have been admitted into the Holy Scriptures, what authority will be left to them? If this be conceded, what sentence can be produced from these Scriptures, by the weight of which the wicked obstinacy of error can be broken down? *Letters* 40.1.

106. Manifestly, therefore, Peter was truly corrected, and Paul has given a true narrative of the event, unless, by the admission of a falsehood here, the authority of the Holy Scriptures given for the faith of all coming generations is to be made wholly uncertain and wavering. For it is neither possible nor suitable to state within the compass of a letter how great and how unutterably evil must be the consequences of such a concession. *Letters* 40.4.

   5. The Bible is inerrant in historical and scientific matters.
      a) *Adam was literally created from dust.*

107. This first man, then, who was formed from the dust of the earth or from slime (since the dust was moistened dust), this "dust of the earth," to use the exact expression of Scripture, became a living body when he received a soul, according to the Apostle's words: "And this man became a living soul." But, it is objected, Adam had a soul already for, otherwise, he would not have been called a man, since a man is not a body only nor a soul only but a being consisting of the two. *City of God* 13.24.

b) Eve was literally created from Adam's rib.

108. The first of all marriages was that between the man made out of dust and his mate who had issued from his side. After that, the continuance and increase of the human race demanded births from the union of males and females, even though there were no other human beings except those born of the first two parents. That is why the men took their sisters. *City of God* 15.16.

109. When God made man according to His own image, He gave him a soul so endowed with reason and intelligence that it ranks man higher than all the other creatures of the earth, the sea, the air, because they lack intelligence. Next, He took a bone from the man's side and made of it a mate to collaborate in procreation. Of course, all this was done in a divine way. If some people take these true facts for mere fables it is because they use familiar, everyday craftsmanship to measure that power and wisdom of God which not merely can but does produce even seeds without seeds. *City of God* 12.24.

c) Patriarchs lived literally hundreds of years.

110. It is now time to examine the evidence which proves convincingly that the Biblical years, so far from being only one-tenth as long as ours, were precisely as long as the present solar years. This is true of the years used in giving those extremely long life-spans. It is said, for example, that the flood occurred in the 600th year of Noe's life. The conclusion is that some men of those ancient times reached an age of more than 900 years and these years were just as long as the years that made up Abraham's age of 170, and his son Isaac's age of 180, and then Jacob's age of nearly 150 and, some time later, Moses' age of 120. . . . *City of God* 15.14.

d) The sun literally stood still for Joshua.

111. Let no man then tell me that the motions of the heavenly bodies are times, because, when at the prayer of one the sun stood still in order that he might achieve his victorious battle, the sun stood still, but time went on. For in such space of time as was sufficient was that battle fought and ended. *Confessions* 11.23.

e) The story of Jonah is literally true.

112. I am much surprised that he reckoned what was done with Jonah to be incredible; unless, perchance, he thinks it easier for a dead man to be raised in life from his sepulchre, than for a living man to be kept in life in the spacious belly of a sea monster. For without mentioning the great size of sea monsters which is reported to us by those who have knowledge of them, let me ask how many men could be contained in the belly which was fenced round with those huge ribs which are fixed in a public place in Carthage, and are well known to all men there? *Letters* 102.31.

113. Let him, therefore, who proposes to inquire why the prophet Jonah was three days in the capacious belly of a sea monster, begin by dismissing doubts as to the fact itself; for this did actually occur, and did not occur in vain. *Letters* 102.33.

C. The Bible refutes the claims of higher criticism.

1. Moses wrote Genesis.

114. Thou placed me in that position that through the service of my heart and of my tongue those books might be distributed, which so long after were to profit all nations, and through the whole world, from so great a pinnacle of authority, were to surmount the words of all false and proud teachings. I should have wished truly had I then been Moses (for we all come from the same mass; and what is man, saving that Thou art mindful of him?). I should then, had I been at that time what he was, and enjoined by Thee to write the book of Genesis, have wished that such a power of expression and such a method of arrangement should be given me, that they who cannot as yet understand how God creates might not reject the words as surpassing their powers. *Confessions* 12.26.

2. Moses was inspired by the Holy Spirit.

115. They are taught, also, by the angels of God who "always behold the face of the Father" and are commissioned to announce His will to others. Among these Prophets was the one who announced in writing: "In the beginning God created the heavens and the earth." And it was so fitting that faith in God should come through such a witness that he was inspired by the same Spirit of God, who had revealed these truths to him, to predict, far in advance, our own future faith. *City of God* 11.4.

3. All miracle stories in the Bible are true.

116. But perhaps our objectors find it impossible to believe in regard to this divine miracle that the heated moist air of the belly, whereby food is dissolved, could be so moderated in temperature as to preserve the life of a man. If so, with how much greater force might they pronounce it incredible that the three young men cast into the furnace by the impious king walked unharmed in the midst of the flames! If, therefore, these objectors refuse to believe any narrative of a divine miracle, they must be refuted by another line of argument. For it is incumbent on them in that case not to single out some one to be objected to, and called in question as incredible, but to denounce as incredible all narratives in which miracles of the same kind or more remarkable are recorded. *Letters* 102.32.

IV. The canonicity of the Bible

A. *The extent of the canon*

1. Augustine numbers the Old Testament books as forty-four.*

117. [The canon of the Old Testament] is contained in the following books:—Five books of Moses, that is, Genesis, Exodus, Leviticus, Numbers, Deuteronomy; one book of Joshua the son of Nun; one of Judges; one short book called Ruth, which seems rather to belong to the beginning of Kings; next, four books of Kings, and two of Chronicles,—these last not following one another, but running parallel, so to speak, and going over the same ground. The books now mentioned are history, which contains a connected narrative of the times, and follows the order of the events. There are other books which seem to follow no regular order, and are connected neither with the order of the preceding books nor with one another, such as Job, and Tobias, and Esther, and Judith, and the two books of Maccabees, and the two of Ezra, which last look more like a sequel to the continuous regular history which terminates with the books of Kings

*He simply numbers the thirty-nine Protestant and eleven Apocryphal books differently. See *a* and *b*.

and Chronicles. Next are the Prophets, in which there is one book of the Psalms of David; and three books of Solomon, viz., Proverbs, Song of Songs, and Ecclesiastes. For two books, one called Wisdom and the other Ecclesiasticus, are ascribed to Solomon from a certain resemblance of style, but the most likely opinion is that they were written by Jesus the son of Sirach. Still they are to be reckoned among the prophetical books, since they have attained recognition as being authoritative. The remainder are the books which are strictly called the Prophets: twelve separate books of the prophets which are connected with one another, and having never been disjoined, are reckoned as one book; the names of these prophets are as follows:—Hosea, Joel, Amos, Obadiah, Jonah, Micah, Nahum, Habakkuk, Zephaniah, Haggai, Zechariah, Malachi; then there are the four greater prophets, Isaiah, Jeremiah, Daniel, Ezekiel. The authority of the Old Testament is contained within the limits of these forty-four books. *On Christian Doctrine* 2.8.

> a) *Lamentations and Baruch are considered part of Jeremiah* (City of God *18.33*).
>
> b) *The four remaining apocryphal books are quoted as part of Daniel and Esther: 1) Addition to Esther* (City of God *18.36*); *2) Hymn of the Three Hebrew Children:* (City of God *11.9*); *3) Bel and the Dragon:* (Correction of the Donatists *4.19*); *4) Susanna:* (Expositions on the Book of Psalms *3.3*).

2. There are twenty-seven books in the New Testament.

118. [The canon] of the New Testament . . . is contained within the following:—Four books of the Gospel, according to Matthew, according to Mark, according to Luke, according to John; fourteen epistles of the Apostle Paul—one to the Romans, two to the Corinthians, one to the Galatians, to the Ephesians, to the Philippians, two to the Thessalonians, one to the Colossians, two to Timothy, one to Titus, to Philemon, to the Hebrews; two of Peter; three of John; one of Jude; and one of James; one book of the Acts of the Apostles; and one of the Revelation of John. *On Christian Doctrine* 2.8.

B. The closing of the canon

119. Nor ought it to appear strange if writings for which so great antiquity is claimed are held in suspicion, seeing that in the very history of the kings of Judah and Israel containing their acts, which we believe to belong to the canonical Scripture, very many things are mentioned which are not explained there, but are said to be found in other books which the prophets wrote, the very names of these prophets being sometimes given, and yet they are not found in the canon which the people of God received. Now I confess the reason of this is hidden from me; only I think that even those men, to whom certainly the Holy Spirit revealed those things which ought to be held as of religious authority, might write some things as men by historical diligence, and others as prophets by divine inspiration; and these things were so distinct, that it was judged that the former should be ascribed to themselves, but the latter to God speaking through them: and so the one pertained to the abundance of knowledge, the other to the authority of religion. In that authority the canon is guarded. So that, if any writings outside of it are now brought forward under the name of the ancient prophets, they cannot serve even as an aid to knowledge, because it is uncertain whether they are genuine; and on this account they are not trusted, especially those of them in which some things are found that are even contrary to the truth of the canonical books, so that it is quite apparent they do not belong to them. *City of God* 18.38.

C. The principles of canonicity

120. 1. Has it been written by a prophet (or apostle)? (See *City of God* 18.38).

121. 2. Does it tell the truth about God? (See *City of God* 18.38).

122. 3. Does it accord with the rest of Scripture? (See *City of God* 18.41).

123. 4. Does it have the authority of God? (See *City of God* 18.38).

124. 5. Has it been accepted by the people of God? (See *Reply to Faustus the Manichaean* 11.5).

125. The authority of these books has come down to us from the apostles through the succession of bishops and the extension of the

Church, and from a position of lofty supremacy, claims the submission of every faithful and pious mind. As regards our writings, which are not a rule of faith or product, but only a help to edification, we may suppose that they contain some things falling short of the truth in obscure and recondite matters. . . . *Reply to Faustus the Manichaean* 11.5.

D. Augustine's mistaken views on the canon

    1. He believed the LXX (the Septuagint,
       containing the Apocrypha) was inspired.

126. When the high priest had sent [the Scriptures] to [Philadelphus] in Hebrew, he afterwards demanded interpreters of him, and there were given him seventy-two, out of each of the twelve tribes six men, most learned in both languages, to wit, the Hebrew and Greek; and their translation is now by custom called the Septuagint. It is reported, indeed, that there was an agreement in their words so wonderful, stupendous, and plainly divine, that when they had sat at this work, each one apart (for so it pleased Ptolemy to test their fidelity), they differed from each other in no word which had the same meaning and force, or, in the other of the words; but, as if the translators had been one, so what all had translated was one, because in very deed the one Spirit had been in them all. And they received so wonderful a gift of God, in order that the authority of these Scriptures might be commended not as human but divine, as indeed it was, for the benefit of the nations who should at some time believe, as we now see them doing. *City of God* 18.42.

    2. He recognized that the Apocrypha was not considered
      part of the Jewish canon but included it anyway.

127. Apart from the errors of copyists, there are discrepancies which may conform to and even emphasize the truth. In such cases, we may well believe that the translators were inspired by the divine Spirit to depart deliberately from the original, for along with their duties as scholars they had rights as prophets. This explains why the Apostles rightly lend their authority not only to the Hebrew text but also to the Septuagint, as when they quote Scriptural texts from the latter. *City of God* 15.14.

E. Augustine's inconsistency on the canon

    1. He held that only prophets could write
      an inspired work.

128. In that authority the canon is guarded. So that, if any writings outside of it are now brought forward under the name of the ancient prophets, they cannot serve even as an aid to knowledge, because it is uncertain whether they are genuine; and on this account they are not trusted, especially those of them in which some things are found that are even contrary to the truth of the canonical books, so that it is quite apparent they do not belong to them. *City of God* 18.38.

    2. Yet he later rejected the Solomonic (i.e., prophetic)
      authorship of the Book of Wisdom; I Maccabees itself
      (9:27) denies being written by a prophet.

129. In the second book, however, with regard to the author of the book which many call the Wisdom of Solomon, I learned later that it is not certain that Jesus, the son of Sirach, wrote this as well as Ecclesiasticus, as I stated; and I found out that it is, indeed, more probable that he is not its author. *Retractations* 1.30.

3

God's Attributes

I. God's nature

A. Aseity

1. God is the absolute Is.

130. It is that absolute "IS," that true "IS," that "IS" in the true sense of the word, that I long for; that "IS;" which "is" in that "Jerusalem" which is "the Bride" of my Lord; where there will not be death, there will not be failing; there will be a day that passeth not away, but continueth: which has neither a yesterday to precede it, nor a to-morrow pressing close upon it. *Expositions on the Book of Psalms* 39.8.

2. God is absolute Being.

131. The conclusion from all this is that God is never to be blamed for any defects that offend us, but should ever be praised for all the perfection we see in the natures He has made. For God is Absolute Being and, therefore, all other being that is relative was made by Him. No being that was made from nothing could be on a par with God, nor could it even be at all, were it not made by Him. *Confessions* 11.5.

3. God is Being Itself.

132. Because I said, "I AM WHO AM," . . . thou didst understand what Being is, and thou hast despaired to grasp it. Take hope, "I am

the God of Abraham, the God of Isaac, and the God of Jacob"; thus I
am what I am, thus I am Being itself, thus I am with Being itself, so
that I may not will to be wanting to men. . . . *Sermons on New
Testament Lessons* 7.7.

4. God is uncreated substance.

133. For all substance that is not a created thing is God, and all that
is not created is God. *On the Trinity* 1.6.

5. God is Supreme Being.

134. Since God is supreme being, that is, since He supremely is and,
therefore, is immutable, it follows that He gave "being" to all that He
created out of nothing; not, however, absolute being. *Confessions*
11.2.

6. God is true Being.

135. Anything whatsoever, no matter how excellent, if it be mutable
has not true being; for true being is not to be found where there is
also non-being. Whatever hath in it the possibility of change, being
changed is not what it was. If that which is not, a kind of death hath
taken place there; something that was there, and is not, has been
destroyed. . . . Something is changed and is that which was not. I see
there a kind of life in that which is, and death in that which has
been. . . . Examine the mutations of things and thou wilt everywhere
find "has been" and "will be." Think on God and thou wilt find "is"
where "has been" and "will be" cannot be. *On the Gospel of John*
38.10.

7. God's existence is more certain than our own.

136. And I said, "Is Truth, therefore, nothing because it is neither
diffused through space, finite, nor infinite?" And Thou criedst to me
from afar, "Yea, verily, 'I AM THAT I AM.'" And I heard this, as things
are heard in the heart, nor was there room for doubt; and I should
more readily doubt that I live than that Truth is not, which is "clearly
seen, being understood by the things that are made." *Confessions*
7.10.

8. We are because God IS.

137. May the Lord therefore console thee, that thou mayest "see the good things of Jerusalem" (Ps. cxxvii, 5). For these good things *are*. Why *are* they? Because they are everlasting. Why *are* they? Because the King is there, I AM WHO AM (Exod. iii, 14). But these good things here are and are not, for they endure not; they slip away, they flow by. AS, p. 90.

B. Immutability

1. God possesses immutability because He possesses aseity.

138. Anything whatsoever, no matter how excellent, if it be mutable has not true *being;* for true being is not to be found where there is also *non-being*. Whatever hath in it the possibility of change, being changed is not what it was. . . . Think on God and thou wilt find "is" where "has been" and "will be" cannot be. *On the Gospel of John* 38.10.

139. Since God is supreme being, that is, since He supremely is and, therefore, is immutable, it follows that He gave being to all that He created out of nothing; not, however, absolute being. To some things He gave more of being and to others less and, in this way, arranged an order of natures in a hierarchy of being. . . . Consequently, no nature—except a non-existent one—can be contrary to the nature which is supreme and which created whatever other natures have being. In other words, nonentity stands in opposition to that which is. Therefore, there is no being opposed to God who is the Supreme Being and Source of all beings without exception. *City of God* 12.2.

2. God's immutability follows from His simplicity.

140. There is, accordingly, a good which alone is simple and, therefore, which alone is unchangeable—and this is God. This good has created all goods; but these are not simple and, therefore, they are mutable. They were created, I repeat, that is, they were made, not begotten. For, what is begotten of the simple good is likewise simple and is what the Begetter is. These two we call the Father and the Son and, together with their Spirit, are one God. *City of God* 11.10.

   3. Immutability means change is impossible.

141. For that which is changed does not retain its own being, and that which can be changed, though it be not actually changed, is able not to be that which it had been. And therefore that which not only is not change, but also is even incapable of being changed at all, alone falls most truly and indubitably under the category of Being. *On the Trinity* 5.2.

   4. Only God is immutable.

142. Now, what makes such evil possible is the fact that no created nature can be immutable. Every such nature is made, indeed, by God, the supreme and immutable Good who made all things good, but, by choosing to sin, such a nature brings evil upon itself. *City of God* 22.1.

143. Thus, there can be no unchangeable good except our one, true, and blessed God. All things which He has made are good because made by Him, but they are subject to change because they were made, not out of Him, but out of nothing. Although they are not supremely good, since God is a greater good than they, these mutable things are, none the less, highly good by reason of their capacity for union with and, therefore, beatitude in the Immutable Good which is so completely their good that, without this good, misery is inevitable. *City of God* 12.1.

   5. God's immutability can be proven
      from a changing world.

144. If there is any loveliness discerned in the lineaments of the body, or beauty in the movement of music and song, it is the mind that makes this judgment. This means that there must be within the mind a superior form, one that is immaterial and independent of sound and space and time. However, the mind itself is not immutable, for, if it were, all minds would judge alike concerning sensible forms. Actually, a clever mind judges more aptly than the stupid one; a skilled one better than one unskilled; an experienced one better than one inexperienced. Even the same mind, once it improves, judges better than it did before.

Undoubtedly, anything susceptible of degrees is mutable, and for this reason, the most able, learned and experienced philosophers readily concluded that the first form of all could not be in any of these things in which the form was clearly mutable. Once they perceived various degrees of beauty in both body and mind, they realized that, if all form were lacking, their very existence would end. Thus, they argued that there must be some reality in which the form was ultimate, immutable and, therefore, not susceptible of degrees. They rightly concluded that only a reality unmade from which all other realities originate could be the ultimate principle of things. *City of God* 8.6.

6. God's will is immutable and eternal.

145. Will you say that these things are false, which, with a strong voice, Truth tells me in my inner ear, concerning the very eternity of the Creator, that His substance is in no wise changed by time, nor that His will is separate from His substance? Wherefore, He willeth not one thing now, another anon, but once and for ever He willeth all things that He willeth; not again and again, nor now this, now that; nor willeth afterwards what He willeth not before, nor willeth not what before He willed. Because such a will is mutable, and no mutable thing is eternal; but our God is eternal. Likewise He tells me, tells me in my inner ear, that the expectation of future things is turned to sight when they have come; and this same sight is turned to memory when they have passed. Moreover, all thought which is thus varied is mutable, and nothing mutable is eternal; but our God is eternal. These things I sum up and put together, and I find that my God, the eternal God, hath not made any creature by any new will, nor that His knowledge suffereth anything transitory. *Confessions* 12.15.

7. God's mind cannot change.

146. For, not in our way does God look forward to the future, see the present, and look back upon the past, but in a manner remotely and profoundly unlike our way of thinking. God's mind does not pass from one thought to another. His vision is utterly unchangeable. Thus, He comprehends all that takes place in time—the not-yet existing future, the existing present, and the no-longer-existing past—in an immutable and eternal present. He does not see differently with the eyes and the mind, for He is not composed of soul and body. Nor is there any then, now, and afterwards in His knowledge, for, unlike ours, it suffers no change with triple time—present, past, and future. With Him, "there is no change, nor shadow of alteration." *City of God* 11.21.

8. God's will is identical with His substance.

147. The will of God, therefore, pertaineth to His very Substance. But if anything hath arisen in the Substance of God which was not before, that Substance is not truly called eternal. *Confessions* 11.10.

9. God is forever identical with Himself.

148. What then is, "the same," save that which is? What is that which is? That which is everlasting. . . . Behold "The Same: I AM THAT I AM, I AM." *Expositions on the Book of Psalms* 122.5.

C. Indivisibility

1. God is one in His essence.

149. From this it follows that neither the whole universe, with its frame, figures, qualities and ordered movement, all the elements and bodies arranged in the heavens and on earth, nor any life . . . can have existence apart from Him whose existence is simple and indivisible. For, in God, being is not one thing and living another—as though He could be and not be living. Nor in God is it one thing to live and another to understand—as though He could live without understanding. Nor in Him is it one thing to know and another to be blessed—as though He could know and not be blessed. For, in God, to live, to know, to be blessed is one and the same as to be. *City of God* 8.6.

2. God is three in His internal relations.

150. The Spirit is other than the Father and the Son because He is neither the Father nor the Son. I say "other than," not "different from," because, equally with them, He is the simple, unchangeable, co-eternal Good. This Trinity is one God. And, although it is a Trinity, it is none the less simple. For, we do not say that the nature of this

good is simple because the Father alone shares in it, or the Son
alone, or the Holy Spirit alone. Nor do we say with the Sabellian
heretics that it is but a nominal Trinity without subsistent Persons.
Our reason for calling it simple is because it is what it has—with the
exception of the real relations in which the Persons stand to each
other. *City of God* 11.10.

> 3. There is no confusion (of persons) or
>   division (in essence) in God.

151. It is, therefore, because we are men, created to the image of a
Creator, whose eternity is true, His truth eternal, His love both eternal
and true, a Creator who is the eternal, true, and lovable Trinity in
whom there is neither confusion nor division, that, wherever we
turn among the things which He created and conserved so wonderfully, we discover His footprints, whether lightly or plainly impressed.
City of God 11.28.

> 4. The Trinity is indivisible in essence.

152. The holy angels gain a knowledge of God not by the spoken
word but by the presence in their souls of that immutable Truth
which is the only-begotten Word of God. They know this Word and
the Father and their Holy Spirit, understanding that this Trinity is
indivisible and that each of the Persons is substantial, although
there are not three Gods but only one. They comprehend all this in
such a way that it is better known to them than we are known to
ourselves. *City of God* 11.29.

153. Let it not be supposed that in this Trinity there is any separation in respect of time or place, but that these Three are equal and
co-eternal, and absolutely of one nature: and that the creatures have
been made, not some by the Father, and some by the Son, and some
by the Holy Spirit, but that each and all that have been or are now
being created subsist in the Trinity as their Creator; and that no one
is saved by the Father without the Son and the Holy Spirit, or by the
Son without the Father and the Holy Spirit, or by the Holy Spirit
without the Father and the Son,—but by the Father, the Son, and the
Holy Spirit, the only one, true, and truly immortal (that is, absolutely
unchangeable) God. *Letters* 169.2.

D. Omnipresence

154. The truth is that all these actions and energies belong to the one true God, who is really a God, who is wholly present everywhere, is confined by no frontiers and bound by no hindrances, is indivisible and immutable, and, though His nature has no need of either heaven or of earth, He fills them both with His presence and His power. *City of God* 7.30.

155. But what is more wonderful than what happens in connection with the sound of our voices and our words, a thing, forsooth, which passes away in a moment? For when we speak, there is no place for even the next syllable till after the preceding one has ceased to sound; nevertheless, if one hearer be present, he hears the whole of what we say, and if two hearers be present, both hear the same, and to each of them it is the whole; and if a multitude listen in silence, they do not break up the sounds like loaves of bread, to be distributed among them individually, but all that is uttered is imparted to all and to each in its entirety. Consider this, and say if it is not more incredible that the abiding Word of God should not accomplish in the universe what the passing word of man accomplishes in the ears of listeners, namely, that as the word of man is present in its entirety to each and all of the hearers, so the Word of God should be present in the entirety of His being at the same moment everywhere. *Letters* 137.2.

E. Omnipotence.

156. We do not put the life of God and the foreknowledge of God under any necessity when we say that God must live an eternal life and must know all things. Neither do we lessen His power when we say He cannot die or be deceived. This is the kind of inability which, if removed, would make God less powerful than He is. God is rightly called omnipotent, even though He is unable to die and be deceived. We call Him omnipotent because He does whatever He wills to do and suffers nothing that He does not will to suffer. He would not, of course, be omnipotent, if He had to suffer anything against His will. It is precisely because He is omnipotent that for Him some things are impossible. *City of God* 5.10.

F. Immateriality

157. The Platonic philosophers, then, so deservedly considered superior to all the others in reputation and achievement, well understood that no body could be God and, therefore, in order to find Him, they rose beyond all material things. Convinced that no mutable reality could be the Most High, they transcended every soul and spirit subject to change in their search for God. They perceived that no determining form by which any mutable being is what it is—whatever be the reality, mode or nature of that form—could have any existence apart from Him who truly exists because His existence is immutable. *City of God* 8.6.

158. Of all visible things, the universe is the greatest; of all invisible realities, the greatest is God. That the world exists we can see; we believe in the existence of God. *City of God* 11.4.

159. This is a matter that I intend to debate with these philosophers later on. Yet we prefer them to all others inasmuch as they agree with us concerning one God, the Creator of the universe, who is not only incorporeal, transcending all corporeal beings, but also incorruptible, surpassing every kind of soul—our source, our light, our goal. *City of God* 8.10.

G. Eternality

1. God possesses eternality because he possesses aseity.

160. What is *the same*, save that which *is?* What is that which *is?* That which is everlasting. For what is always different at different times, is not, because it abideth not. Not that it altogether is not, but is not in the highest sense. And what is that which *is*, save He who when He sent Moses, said unto him, I AM WHO AM (Exod. iii, 14)? *Expositions on the Book of Psalms* 121.5.

2. *Eternal God* means He ever was, is, and will be.

161. God always is, nor has He been and is not, nor is but has not been, but as He never will not be; so He never was not. *On the Trinity* 14.15.

3. God alone is eternal.

162. I have no doubt either that the soul is immortal—not in the same sense in which God is immortal, who alone hath immortality, but in a certain way peculiar to itself—or that the soul is a creature and not a part of the substance of the Creator, or as to any other thing which I regard as most certain concerning its nature. *Letters* 143.7.

4. God's will is eternal and unchangeable.

163. Already hast Thou told me, O Lord, with a strong voice, in my inner ear, that Thou art eternal, having alone immortality. Since Thou art not changed by any shape or motion, nor is Thy will altered by times, because no will which changes is immortal. *Confessions* 12.11.

II. God's relation to time

A. *The nature of time*

1. What time is

164. The distinguishing mark between time and eternity is that the former does not exist without some movement and change, while in the latter there is no change at all. Obviously, then, there could have been no time had not a creature been made whose movement would effect some change. It is because the parts of this motion and change cannot be simultaneous, since one part must follow another, that, in these shorter or longer intervals of duration, time begins. Now, since God, in whose eternity there is absolutely no change, is the Creator and Ruler of time, I do not see how we can say that He created the world after a space of time had elapsed unless we admit, also, that previously some creature had existed whose movements would mark the course of time. *City of God* 11.6.

165. Whence it appeared to me that time is nothing else than protraction; but of what I know not. It is wonderful to me, if it be not of the mind itself. For what do I measure, I beseech Thee, O my God, even when I say either indefinitely, "This time is longer than that;" or even definitely, "This is double that?" That I measure time, I know. But I measure not the future, for it is not yet; nor do I measure the present, because it is extended by no space; nor do I measure the past, because it no longer is. What, therefore, do I measure? Is it times passing, not past? For thus had I said. *Confessions* 11.26.

166. In thee, O my mind, I measure times. Do not overwhelm me with thy clamour. That is, do not overwhelm thyself with the multitude of thy impressions. In thee, I say, I measure times; the impression which things as they pass by make on Thee, and which, when they have passed by, remains, that I measure as time present, not those things which I have passed by, that the impression should be made. This I measure when I measure times. Either, then, these are times, or I do not measure times. What when we measure silence, and say that this silence hath lasted as long as that voice lasts? Do we not extend our thought to the measure of a voice, as if it sounded, so that we may be able to declare something concerning the intervals of silence in a given space of time? For when both the voice and tongue are still, we go over in thought poems and verses, and any discourse, or dimensions of motions; and declare concerning the spaces of times, how much this may be in respect of that, not otherwise than if uttering them we should pronounce them. Should any one wish to utter a lengthened sound, and had with forethought determined how long it should be, that man hath in silence verily gone through a space of time, and, committing it to memory, he begins to utter that speech, which sounds until it be extended to the end proposed; truly it hath sounded, and will sound. For what of it is already finished hath verily sounded, but what remains will sound; and thus does it pass on, until the present intention carry over the future into the past; the past increasing by the diminution of the future, until, by the consumption of the future, all be past. *Confessions* 11.27.

167. But as yet it sounds, nor can it be measured, save from that instant in which it began to sound, even to the end in which it left off. For the interval itself we measure from some beginning unto some end. On which account, a voice which is not yet ended cannot be measured, so that it may be said how long or how short it may be; nor can it be said to be equal to another, or single or double in respect of it, or the like. But when it is ended, it no longer is. *Confessions* 11.27.

2. What time is not

168. I have heard from a learned man that the motions of the sun, moon, and stars constituted time, and I assented not. For why should not rather the motions of all bodies be time? What if the lights of heaven should cease, and a potter's wheel run round, would there be no time by which we might measure those revolutions, and say either that it turned with equal pauses, or, if it were moved at one time more slowly, at another more quickly, that some revolutions were longer, others less so? *Confessions* 11.23.

3. How time is measured

169. By common sense, then, I measure a long by a short syllable, and I find that it has twice as much. But when one sounds after another, if the former be short the latter long, how shall I hold the short one, and how measuring shall I apply it to the long, so that I may find out that this has twice as much, when indeed the long does not begin to sound unless the short leaves off sounding? That very long one I measure not as present, since I measure it not save when ended. But its ending is its passing away. What, then, is it that I can measure? Where is the short syllable by which I measure? Where is the long one which I measure? Both have sounded, have flown, have passed away, and are no longer; and still I measure, and I confidently answer (so far as is trusted to a practised sense), that as to space of time this syllable is single, that double. Nor could I do this, unless because they have past, and are ended. Therefore do I not measure themselves, which now are not, but something in my memory, which remains fixed. *Confessions* 11.27.

170. Let us therefore see, O human soul, whether present time can be long; for to thee is it given to perceive and to measure periods of time. What wilt thou reply to me? Is a hundred years when present a long time? See, first, whether a hundred years can be present. For if the first year of these is current, that is present, but the other ninety and nine are future, and therefore they are not as yet. But if the second year is current, one is already past, the other present, the rest future. And thus, if we fix on any middle year of this hundred as present, those before it are past, those after it are future; wherefore a hundred years cannot be present. See at least whether that year itself which is current can be present. For if its first month be current, the rest are future; if the second, the first hath already passed, and the remainder are not yet. Therefore neither is the year which is current as a whole present; and if it is not present as a whole, then the year is not present. For twelve months make the year, of which each individual month which is current is itself present, but the rest are either past or future. Although neither is that month which is current present, but one day only: if the first, the rest being to come, if the last, the rest being past; if any of the middle, then between past and future. *Confessions* 11.15.

4. When time is measured

171. Wherefore, as I said, we measure times as they pass. And if any one should ask me, "Whence dost thou know?" I can answer, "I know, because we measure; nor can we measure things that are not; and things past and future are not." But how do we measure present time, since it hath not space? It is measured while it passeth; but when it shall have passed, it is not measured; for there will not be aught that can be measured. But whence, in what way, and whither doth it pass while it is being measured? Whence, but from the future? Which way, save through the present? Whither, but into the past? From that, therefore, which as yet is not, through that which hath no space, into that which now is not. But what do we measure, unless time in some space? For we say not single, and double, and triple, and equal, or in any other way in which we speak of time, unless with respect to the spaces of times. In what space, then, do we measure passing time? Is it in the future, whence it passeth over? But what yet we measure not, is not. Or is it in the present, by which it passeth? But no space we do not measure. Or in the past, whither it passeth? But that which is not now, we measure not. *Confessions* 11.21.

172. But we measure times passing when we measure them by perceiving them; but past times, which now are not, or future times, which as yet are not, who can measure them? Unless, perchance, any one will dare to say, that that can be measured which is not. When, therefore, time is passing, it can be perceived and measured; but when it has passed, it cannot, since it is not. *Confessions* 11.16.

5. Time and eternity compared

173. Those who say these things do not as yet understand Thee, O Thou Wisdom of God, Thou light of souls; not as yet do they understand how these things be made which are made by and in Thee. They even endeavour to comprehend things eternal; but as yet their heart flieth about in the past and future motions of things, and is still wavering. Who shall hold it and fix it, that it may rest a little, and by degrees catch the glory of that ever-standing eternity, and compare it with the times which never stand, and see that it is incomparable; and that a long time cannot become long, save from the many motions that pass by, which cannot at the same instant be prolonged; but that in the Eternal nothing passeth away, but that the whole is present; but no time is wholly present; and let him see that all time past is forced on by the future, and that all the future followeth from the past, and that all, both past and future, is created and issues from that which is always present? Who will hold the heart of man, that it may stand still, and see how the still-standing eternity, itself neither future nor past, uttereth the times future and past? Can my hand accomplish this, or the hand of my mouth by persuasion bring about a thing so great? *Confessions* 11.11.

B. The relation of time and the act of creation

1. Only God can create.

174. Rarely and only with great effort does a mind, which has contemplated both the material and spiritual creation of the universe and discovered the mutability of all things, soar to the unchangeable substance of God and there learn that He is the sole Creator of every nature that is not divine. *City of God* 11.2.

175. The word "form" has two meanings. Every material body has an outer form shaped by a potter, or smith, or other artisan who can paint or fashion even forms that look like the shapes of animals. But there is also an inner form which is not a shape but a shaper, with an efficient causality deriving from the secret and hidden determination of some living and intelligent nature which can shape not merely the outer forms of physical bodies but the inner souls of living things. The first kind of form we may attribute to any artificer, but the second, only to the one Artificer, Creator and Maker, who is God. *City of God* 12.26.

2. The world was not created from eternity.

176. There are those who say that the universe was, indeed, created by God, denying a "temporal" but admitting a "creational" beginning, as though, in some hardly comprehensible way, the world was made, but made from all eternity. Their purpose seems to be to save God from the charge of arbitrary rashness. They would not have us believe that a completely new idea of creating the world suddenly occurred to Him or that a change of mind took place in Him in whom there can be no change.

I do not see, however, how this position is consistent with their stand in other matters, especially in regard to the soul. For, if, as they must hold, the soul is co-eternal with God, they have no way to explain how a completely new misery can begin in an eternally existing soul. *City of God* 11.4.

177. Before attempting to reply to those who, while agreeing with us that God is the Creator of the world, question us about the time at which it was created, we must see what response they make when we ask them about the space in which it was created. For, just as they ask why it was made then and not earlier, we may ask why it was made here and not elsewhere. Because, if they excogitate infinite periods of time before the world, in which they cannot see how God could have had nothing to do, they ought to conceive of infinite reaches of space beyond the visible universe. And, if they maintain that the Omnipotent can never be inactive, will they not logically be forced to dream with Epicurus of innumerable universes? (There will be merely this difference, that, while he asserts that these worlds originate and disintegrate by the fortuitous movements of atoms, they will hold that they are created by the work of God.) This is the conclusion if they insist on the premise that there is an interminable immensity of space stretching in all directions in which God cannot remain passive and that those imaginary worlds, like this visible one, are indestructible. *City of God* 11.5.

178. At no time, therefore, hadst Thou not made anything, because Thou hadst made time itself. And no times are co-eternal with Thee, because Thou remainest for ever. . . . *Confessions* 11.14.

179. Finally, if they say that the soul was created in time but will not perish in any future time, like numbers which begin with "one" but never end, and, therefore, that having experienced misery, it will be freed from it, never again to return to it, they will surely have no hesitation in admitting that this is compatible with the immutability of God's decision. This being so, they should also believe that the world could be made in time without God who made it having to change the eternal decision of His will. *City of God* 11.4.

3. The world was not created out of God.

180. For Thou didst create heaven and earth, not out of Thyself, for then they would be equal to Thine Only-begotten, and thereby even to Thee; and in no wise would it be right that anything should be equal to Thee which was not of Thee. *Confessions* 12.7.

181. Nor didst Thou hold anything in Thy hand wherewith to make heaven and earth. For whence couldest Thou have what Thou hast not made, whereof to make anything? For what is, save because Thou are? Therefore Thou didst speak and they were made, and in Thy word Thou madest these things. *Confessions* 11.5.

4. The world was created *ex nihilo*.

182. And aught else except Thee there was not whence Thou mightest create these things, O God, One Trinity, and Trine Unity; and, therefore, out of nothing didst Thou create heaven and earth,— a great thing and a small,—because Thou are Almighty and Good, to make all things good, even the great heaven and the small earth. Thou wast, and there was nought else from which Thou didst create heaven and earth; two such things, one near unto Thee, the other near to nothing,—one to which Thou shouldest be superior, the other to which nothing should be inferior. *Confessions* 12.7.

5. Time did not always exist.

a) *Time was created with the world.*

183. Again, sacred and infallible Scripture tells us that in the beginning God created heaven and earth in order. Now, unless this meant that nothing had been made before, it would have been stated that whatever else God had made before was created in the beginning.

Undoubtedly, then, the world was made not in time but together with time. For, what is made in time is made after one period of time and before another, namely, after a past and before a future time. But, there could have been no past time, since there was nothing created by whose movements and change time could be measured.

The fact is that the world was made simultaneously with time, if, with creation, motion and change began. Now this seems evident from the order of the first six or seven days. For, the morning and evening of each of these days are counted until on the sixth day all that had been created during this time was complete. *City of God* 11.6.

184. For whence could innumerable ages pass by which Thou didst not make, since Thou are the Author and Creator of all ages? Or what times should those be which were not made by Thee? Or how should they pass by if they had not been? Since, therefore, Thou art the Creator of all times, if any time was before Thou madest heaven and earth, why is it said that Thou didst refrain from working? For that very time Thou madest, nor could times pass by before Thou madest times. But if before heaven and earth there was no time, why is it asked, What didst Thou then? For there was no "then" when time was not. *Confessions* 11.13.

b) Time did not exist before the world existed.

185. Obviously, then, we should acknowledge that God alone is the Founder of every nature. In His creation, He uses no material and no workmen which He Himself has not made. And if He were to withdraw, so to speak, His building power from creatures, they would no more exist than they existed before they were created. The "before," of course, refers not to time but to eternity. For He alone could be the Creator of time who created those things whose motions are the measure of time. *City of God* 12.26.

186. Nor dost Thou by time precede time; else wouldest not Thou precede all times. But in the excellency of an ever-present eternity, Thou precedest all times past, and survivest all future times, because they are future, and when they have come they will be past; but "Thou art the same, and Thy years shall have no end." Thy years neither go nor come; but ours both go and come, that all may come.

All Thy years stand at once since they do stand; nor were they when departing excluded by coming years, because they pass not away; but all these of ours shall be when all shall cease to be. Thy years are one day, and Thy day is not daily, but to-day; because Thy to-day yields not with to-morrow, for neither doth it follow yesterday. *Confessions* 11.13.

187. But Thou, O Lord, who ever livest, and in whom nothing dies (since before the world was, and indeed before all that can be called "before," Thou existest, and art the God and Lord of all Thy creatures; and with Thee fixedly abide the causes of all unstable things, the unchanging sources of all things changeable, and the eternal reasons of all things unreasoning and temporal), tell me, Thy suppliant, O God. *Confessions* 1.6.

6. God did not create the world within the framework of time.

a) *What did God do before He created the world?*

188. Of course, they may admit that it is silly to imagine infinite space since there is no such thing as space beyond the cosmos. In that case, let this be the answer: It is silly for them to excogitate a past time during which God was unoccupied, for the simple reason that there was no such thing as time before the universe was made. *City of God* 11.5.

189. And I will be immoveable, and fixed in Thee, in my mould, Thy truth; nor will I endure the questions of men, who by a penal disease thirst for more than they can hold, and say, "What did God make before He made heaven and earth?" Or, "How came it into His mind to make anything, when He never before made anything?" Grant to them, O Lord, to think well what they say, and to see that where there is no time, they cannot say "never." What, therefore, He is said "never to have made," what else is it but to say, that in no time was it made? Let them therefore see that there could be no time without a created being, and let them cease to speak that vanity. Let them also be extended unto those things which are before, and understand that Thou, the eternal Creator of all times, art before all times, and that no times are co-eternal with Thee, nor any creature, even if there be any creature beyond all times. *Confessions* 11.30.

b) Why did not God create sooner?

190. But, why did it please the eternal God to create heaven and earth at that special time, seeing that He had not done so earlier? If the purpose of those who pose this question is to protest that the world is eternal, without beginning, and, therefore, not created by God, then they are far from the truth and are raving with the deadly disease of irreligion. For, quite apart from the voice of the Prophets, the very order, changes, and movements in the universe, the very beauty of form in all that is visible, proclaim, however silently, both that the world was created and also that its Creator could be none other than God whose greatness and beauty are both ineffable and invisible. *City of God* 11.4.

c) Could God have created in a shorter time?

191. It is recorded that all God's works were completed in six days (the day being repeated six times), because six is a perfect number. Of course, no prolongation of time was necessary for God. He could have at once created all things and then let them measure time by their appropriate movements. *City of God* 11.30.

C. God's knowledge of time

1. God does not see things in time.

192. Unto these things Thou repliest unto me, for Thou art my God, and with a strong voice tellest unto Thy servant in his inner ear, bursting through my deafness, and crying, "O man, that which My Scripture saith, I say; and yet doth that speak in time; but time has no reference to My Word, because My Word existeth in equal eternity with Myself. Thus those things which ye see through My Spirit, I see, just as those things which ye speak through My Spirit, I speak. And so when ye see those things in time, I see them not in time; as when ye speak them in time, I speak them not in time." *Confessions* 13.29.

2. God does not see things as they come to pass.

193. O Lord, since eternity is Thine, art Thou ignorant of the things which I say unto Thee? Or seest Thou at the time that which cometh to pass in time? Why, therefore, do I place before Thee so many relations of things? Not surely that Thou mightest know them through me, but that I may awaken my own love and that of my readers towards Thee, that we may all say, "Great is the Lord, and greatly to be praised." *City of God* 11.1.

3. God knows independently of time.

194. Neither does His attention pass from thought to thought, for His knowledge embraces everything in a single spiritual contuition. His knowledge of what happens in time, like His movement of what changes in time, is completely independent of time. That is why it was one and the same to God to see that what He had made was good and to see that it was good to make it. When He saw what He had made, His knowledge was neither doubled nor in any way increased—in the sense that it could have been less before He made what He saw. For He could not have been so perfect a Creator without so perfect a knowledge that nothing could be added to it by seeing what He created. *City of God* 11.21.

4. God sees all time as one.

195. Surely, if there be a mind, so greatly abounding in knowledge and foreknowledge, to which all things past and future are so known as one psalm is well known to me, that mind is exceedingly wonderful, and very astonishing; because whatever is so past, and whatever is to come of after ages, is no more concealed from Him than was it hidden from me when singing that psalm, what and how much of it had been sung from the beginning, what and how much remained unto the end. But far be it that Thou, the Creator of the universe, the Creator of souls and bodies,—far be it that Thou shouldest know all things future and past. Far, far more wonderfully, and far more mysteriously, Thou knowest them. For it is not as the feelings of one singing known things, or hearing a known song, are—through expectation of future words, and in remembrance of those that are past—varied, and his senses divided, that anything happeneth unto Thee, unchangeably eternal, that is, the truly eternal Creator of minds. As, then, Thou in the Beginning knewest the heaven and the earth without any change of Thy knowledge, so in the Beginning didst Thou make heaven and earth without any distraction of Thy action. *City of God* 11.31.

    5. God sees all of time in the present.

196. In the eternal nothing passeth away, but that the whole is present . . . all, both past and future, is created and issues from that which is always present? *Confessions* 11.11.

197. For the years of God, and God Himself, are not different: but the years of God are the eternity of God: eternity is the very substance of God, which hath nothing changeable; there nothing is past, as if it were no longer: nothing is future, as if it existed not as yet. There is nothing there but, Is: there is not there, Was, and Will be; because what was, is now no longer: and what will be, is not as yet: but whatever is there, simply Is. . . . Behold this great I AM! *Expositions on the Book of Psalms* 102.27.

D. God's will and time

198. And so when ye see those things in time, I see them not in time; and when ye speak them in time, I speak them not in time. *Confessions* 13.29.

199. Thou callest us, therefore, to understand the Word, God with Thee, God, which is spoken eternally, and by it are all things spoken eternally. For what was spoken was not finished, and another spoken until all were spoken; but all things at once and for ever. For otherwise have we time and change, and not a true eternity, nor a true immortality. *Confessions* 11.7.

E. God's acts and time

200. Lo, are they not full of their ancient way, who say to us, "What was God doing before He made heaven and earth? For if," say they, "He were unoccupied, and did nothing, why does He not for ever also, and from henceforth, cease from working, as in times past He did? For if any new motion has arisen in God, and a new will, to form a creature which He had never before formed, however can that be a true eternity where there ariseth a will which was not before? For the will of God is not a creature, but before the creature; because nothing could be created unless the will of the Creator were before it? . . ." Those who say these things do not as yet understand Thee. . . .

They even endeavor to comprehend things eternal; but as yet their heart flieth about in the past and future motions of things, and is still wavering. Who shall hold it and fix it, that it may rest a little, and by degrees catch the glory of the ever-standing eternity and compare it with the times which never stand, and see that it is incomparable. . . . *Confessions* 11.10,11.

4

Christ

I. Humanity: Christ as man

A. *Christ's human nature was full and complete.*

201. Therefore here also let us perceive the Lord's Passion, and let there speak to us Christ, Head and Body. So always, or nearly always, let us hear the words of Christ from the Psalm, as that we look not only upon that Head, the one mediator between God and man, the Man Christ Jesus. . . . But let us think of Christ, Head and whole Body, a sort of entire Man. For to us is said, "But ye are the Body of Christ and members," by the Apostle Paul. *Expositions on the Book of Psalms* 59.2.

  1. Christ was one of the children of men.

202. Lo! now then that Word, so uttered, Eternal, the Co-eternal Offspring of the Eternal, will come as "the Bridegroom;" "Fairer than the children of men" (ver. 2); "Than the children of men." I ask, why not then the Angels also? Why did he say, "than the children of men," except because He was "Man," he is "fairer than the children of men;" though among the children of men, "fairer than the children of men:" though of the children of men. *Expositions on the Book of Psalms* 45.7.

  2. Christ "assumed flesh" through the Virgin Mary.

203. This people, I say, added to those who are the true Israelites both by the flesh and by faith, is the city of God, which has brought forth Christ Himself according to the flesh, since He was in these Israelites only. For thence came the Virgin Mary, in whom Christ assumed flesh that He might be man. Of which city another psalm says, "Mother Sion, shall a man say, and the man is made in her, and the Highest Himself hath founded her." Who is this Highest, save God? And thus Christ, who is God, before He became man through Mary in that city, Himself founded it by the patriarchs and prophets. *City of God* 17.16.

a) The term assuming flesh *does not mean "made into flesh."*

204. For who will explain in consistent words this single statement, that "the Word was made flesh, and dwelt among us," so that we may believe on the only Son of God the Father Almighty, born of the Holy Ghost and the Virgin Mary? The meaning of the Word being made flesh, is not that the divine nature was changed into flesh, but that the divine nature assumed our flesh. *Enchiridion* 34.

b) Christ's body was wholly free from any taint of sin.

205. For we must believe that no part was wanting in that human nature which He put on, save that it was a nature wholly free from every taint of sin,—not such a nature as is conceived between the two sexes through carnal lust, which is born in sin, and whose guilt is washed away in regeneration; but such as it behoved a virgin to bring forth, when the mother's flesh, not her lust, was the condition of conception. *Enchiridion* 34.

c) Christ, however, did voluntarily assume a mortal body.

206. The animal body is the first, being such as the first Adam had, and which would not have died had he not sinned, being such also as we now have, its nature being changed and vitiated by sin to the extent of bringing us under the necessity of death, and being such as even Christ condescended first of all to assume, not indeed of necessity, but of choice; but afterwards comes the spiritual body, which already is worn by anticipation by Christ as our head, and will be worn by His members in the resurrection of the dead. *City of God* 13.23.

d) Christ assumed, within Mary's womb, all of human nature.

207. But whereas, in a temporal dispensation, as I have said, with a view to our salvation and restoration, and with the goodness of God acting therein, our changeable nature has been assumed by the unchangeable Wisdom of God, we add the faith in temporal things which have been done with salutary effect on our behalf, believing in that Son of God WHO WAS BORN THROUGH THE HOLY GHOST OF THE VIRGIN MARY. For by the gift of God, that is, by the Holy Spirit there was granted to us so great humility on the part of so great a God, that He deemed it worthy of Him to assume the entire nature of man (*totum hominem*) in the womb of the Virgin, inhabiting the material body so that it sustained no detriment (*integrum*), and leaving it without detriment. *On Faith and the Creed* 8.

> *e) But Mary was not the mother of Christ's divine nature.*

208. But He rather admonishes us to understand that, in respect of His being God, there was no mother for Him, the part of whose personal majesty (*cujus majestatis personam*) He was preparing to show forth in the turning of water into wine. *On Faith and the Creed* 9.

> *f) The assumption of flesh honored both sexes.*

209. Moreover, those parties also are to be abhorred who deny that our Lord Jesus Christ had in Mary a mother upon earth; while that dispensation has honored both sexes, at once the male and female, and has made it plain that not only that sex which He assumed pertains to God's care, but also that sex by which He did assume this other, in that He bore [the nature of] the man (*virum gerendo*), [and] in that He was born of the woman. *On Faith and the Creed* 9.

> *g) The assumption of flesh united both the divine and*
> *human natures.*

210. For when He was the only Son of God, not by grace, but by nature, that He might be also full of grace. He became the Son of man; and He Himself unites both natures in His own identity, and both natures constitute one Christ; because, "being in the form of God, He thought it not robbery to be," what He was by nature, "equal with God." But He made Himself of no reputation, and took upon Himself the form of a servant, not losing or lessening the form of God. And, accordingly, He was both made less and remained equal, being both in one, as has been said: but He was one of these as Word, and the other as man. *Enchiridion* 35.

   3. Christ as man demonstrated human frailty.

211. The fact that He took rest in sleep, and was nourished by food, and experienced all the feelings of humanity, is the evidence to men of the reality of that human nature which He assumed but did not destroy. *Letters* 137.3.

a) Human frailty was demonstrated in His emotions.

212. For as there was in Him a true human body and a true human soul, so was there also a true human emotion. When, therefore, we read in the Gospel that the hardheartedness of the Jews moved Him to sorrowful indignation, that He said, "I am glad for your sakes, to the intent ye may believe," that when about to raise Lazarus He even shed tears, that He earnestly desired to eat the passover with His disciples, that as His passion drew near His soul was sorrowful, these emotions are certainly not falsely ascribed to Him. But as He became man when it pleased Him, so, in the grace of His definite purpose, when it pleased Him He experienced those emotions in His human soul. *City of God* 14.9.

b) Human frailty was demonstrated in the crucifixion of His body.

213. But as regards His being crucified, He was crucified in respect of his being man; and that was the *hour* which had not come as yet, at the time when this word was spoken, "What have I to do with thee? Mine hour is not yet come:" that is, the hour at which I shall recognize thee. For at that period, when He was crucified as man, He recognized His human mother (*humanum matrem*), and committed her most humanely (*humanissime*) to the care of the best beloved disciple. *On Faith and the Creed* 9.

   4. Christ as man set the example for men.

214. But as "the Word was made flesh, and dwelt among us," the same Wisdom which was begotten of God condescended also to be created among men. There is a reference to this in the Word, "The Lord created me in the beginning of His ways." For the beginning of His ways is the Head of the Church, which is Christ endued with human nature (*homine indutus*), by whom it was purposed that there should be given to us a pattern of living, that is, a sure way by which we might reach God. *On Faith and the Creed* 6.

5. Christ as man was sinless.

215. Whosoever, then, supposes that any man or any men (except the one Mediator between God and man) have ever lived, or are yet living in this present state, who have not needed, and do not need, forgiveness of sins, he opposes Holy Scripture, wherein it is said by the apostle: "By one man sin entered into the world, and death by sin; and so death passed upon all men, in which all have sinned." *On Man's Perfection in Righteousness* 21.

216. Finally, . . . it [is] asserted that there [n]either have been [n]or are in this present life, any persons, with the sole exception of our Great Head, "the Saviour of His body," who are righteous, without any sin. . . . *On Man's Perfection in Righteousness* 21.

6. Christ as man was inferior to the Father.

217. Therefore the apostle does not say, "There is one Mediator between God and men, even Jesus Christ;" but his words are, "The MAN Christ Jesus." He is the Mediator, then, in that He is man,— inferior to the Father, by so much as He is nearer to ourselves, and superior to us, by so much as He is nearer to the Father. This is more openly expressed thus: "He is inferior to the Father, because in the form of a servant;" superior to us, because without spot of sin. *On Original Sin* 33.

B. Christ's human nature was necessary for our salvation.

218. But how are we reconciled, save by the removal of that which separates between us and Himself? For He says by the prophet, "he hath not made the ear heavy that it should not hear; but your iniquities have separated between you and your God." And so, then, we are not reconciled, unless that which is in the midst is taken away, and something else is put in its place. For there is a separating medium, and, on the other hand, there is a reconciling Mediator. The separating medium is sin, the reconciling Mediator is the Lord Jesus Christ; "For there is one God and Mediator between God and men, the man Christ Jesus." To take then away the separating wall, which is sin, that Mediator has come, and the priest has Himself become the sacrifice. *On the Gospel of John* 41.5.

1. Christ the mediator between God and man

219. If He preacheth Himself, and by preaching entereth into thee, He entereth into thee by Himself. And He is the door to the Father, for there is no way of approach to the Father but by Him. "For there is one God and one Mediator between God and men, the man Christ Jesus." *On the Gospel of John* 47.3.

2. The necessity of Christ's mediation

220. And as the things beneath, which are mortal and impure, cannot hold intercourse with the immortal purity which is above, a mediator is indeed needed to remove this difficulty; but not a mediator who resembles the highest order of being by possessing an immortal body, and the lowest by having a diseased soul, which makes him rather grudge that we be healed than help our cure. *City of God* 9.17.

221. We need a Mediator who, being united to us here below the morality of His body, should at the same time be able to afford us truly divine help in cleansing and liberating us by means of the immortal righteousness of His spirit, whereby He remained heavenly even while here upon earth. *City of God* 9.17.

222. For "there is one God, and one Mediator between God and men, the man Christ Jesus;" since "there is none other name under heaven given to men, whereby we must be saved;" and "in Him hath God defined unto all men their faith, in that He hath raised Him from the dead." Now without this faith, that is to say, without a belief in the one Mediator between God and men, the man Christ Jesus; without faith, I say, in His resurrection, by which God has given assurance to all men, and which no man could of course truly believe, were it not for His incarnation and death; without faith, therefore, in the incarnation and death and resurrection of Christ, the Christian verity unhesitatingly declares that the ancient saints could not possibly have been cleansed from sin, so as to have become holy, and justified by the grace of God. *On Original Sin* 28.

3. The purpose of Christ's mediation

a) Immortality

223. Now we bear the image of the earthly man by the propagation of sin and death, which pass on to us by ordinary generation; but we bear the image of the heavenly by the grace of pardon and life eternal, which regeneration confers upon us through the Mediator of God and men, the Man Christ Jesus. And He is the heavenly Man of Paul's passage, because He came from heaven to be clothed with a body of earthly mortality, that He might clothe it with heavenly immortality. And he calls others heavenly, because by grace they become His members, that, together with them, He may become one Christ, as head and body. *City of God* 13.23.

b) Reconciliation

224. Wherefore the apostle says: "For if, when we were enemies, we were reconciled to God by the death of His Son, much more, being reconciled, we shall be saved by His life." Now when God is said to be angry, we do not attribute to Him such a disturbed feeling as exists in the mind of an angry man; but we call His just displeasure against sin by the name "anger," a word transferred by analogy from human emotions. But our being reconciled to God through a Mediator, and receiving the Holy Spirit, so that we who were enemies are made sons ("For as many as are led by the Spirit of God, they are the sons of God"): this is the grace of God through Jesus Christ our Lord. *Enchiridion* 36.

c) Salvation

225. And, nevertheless, "although He was in the same form, He emptied Himself, taking the form of a servant,"—and so on down to the words "the death of the cross." What is the explanation of this but that He made Himself "weak to the weak, in order that He might gain the weak?" Listen to His follower as he expresses himself also in another place to this effect: "For whether we be beside ourselves, it is to God; or whether we be sober, it is for your cause. For the love of Christ constraineth us, because we thus judge that He died for all." *On the Catechising of the Uninstructed* 10.15.

C. Christ as man is the second Adam.

226. Nevertheless, that one sin, admitted into a place where such perfect happiness reigned, was of so heinous a character, that in one man the whole human race was originally, and as one may say, radically, condemned; and it cannot be pardoned and blotted out except through the one Mediator between God and men, that man Christ Jesus, who only has had power to be so born as not to need a second birth. *Enchiridion* 48.

D. Christ as man necessitates the resurrection of the dead.

227. "For the sin of the first transgressor could not possibly have injured us more than the incarnation or redemption of the Saviour has benefited us." But why do they not rather give an attentive ear, and an unhesitating belief, to that which the apostle has stated so unambiguously: "Since by man came death, by Man came also the resurrection of the dead; for as in Adam all die, even so in Christ shall all be made alive?" For it is of nothing else than of the resurrection of the body that he was speaking. Having said that the bodily death of all men has come about through one man, he adds the promise that the bodily resurrection of all men to eternal life shall happen through one, even Christ. *On Forgiveness of Sins, and Baptism* 2.49.

E. Christ as man judges man on the basis of His humanity.

228. "The Father judgeth no man, but hath committed all judgment unto the Son;" as if it were said, No one will see the Father in the judgment of the quick and the dead, but all will see the Son: because He is also the Son of man, so that he can be seen even by the ungodly, since they too shall see Him whom they have pierced. *On the Trinity* 1.13.

II. Deity: Christ as God

A. *Christ's divine nature is full and complete.*

1. Christ as God is coequal with the Father.

229. But our Lord Jesus Christ has shown us a great example of humility: for doubtless He is equal with the Father, for "in the beginning was the Word, and the Word was with God, and the Word was God;" yea, doubtless, He Himself said, and most truly said, "Am I so long time with you, and ye have not known me, Philip? He that hath seen me hath seen the Father." Yea, doubtless, Himself said, and most truly said, "I and the Father are one." If, therefore, He is one with the Father, equal to the Father, God from God, God with God, co-eternal, immortal, alike without time, alike Creator and disposer of times; and yet because He came in time, and took the form of a servant, and in condition was found as a man, He seeks the glory of the Father, not His own; what oughtest thou to do, O man, who, when thou doest anything good, seekest thy own glory; but when thou doest anything ill, dost meditate calumny against God? *On the Gospel of John* 29.8.

230. For that before all times, and above all times, Thy only-begotten Son remaineth unchangeably co-eternal with Thee; and that of "His fulness" souls receive, that they may be blessed; and that by participation of the wisdom remaining in them they are renewed, that they may be wise, is there. *Confessions* 7.9.

231. They who have said that our Lord Jesus Christ is not God, or not very God, or not with the Father the One and only God, or not truly immortal because changeable, are proved wrong by the most plain and unanimous voice of divine testimonies; as, for instance, "In the beginning was the Word, and the Word was with God, and the Word was God." For it is plain that we are to take the Word of God to be the only Son of God, of whom it is afterwards said, "And the Word was made flesh, and dwelt among us," on account of that birth of His incarnation, which was wrought in time of the Virgin. *On the Trinity* 1.6.

2. Christ as God is coeternal with the Father and Spirit:
   a Trinity.

232. The divine generation, therefore, of our Lord, and his human dispensations, having both been thus systematically disposed and commended to faith, there is added to our Confession, with a view to the perfecting of the faith which we have regarding God, [the doctrine of] THE HOLY SPIRIT, who is not of a nature inferior to the Father and the Son, but, so to say, consubstantial and co-eternal: for this Trinity is one God, not to the effect that the Father is the same [Person] as the Son and the Holy Spirit, but to the effect that the Father is the Father, and the Son is the Son, and the Holy Spirit is the Holy Spirit; and this Trinity is the one God, according as it is written, "Hear, O Israel, the Lord your God is one God." *On Faith and the Creed* 9.

233. All those Catholic expounders of the divine Scriptures, both Old and New, whom I have been able to read, who have written before me concerning the Trinity, Who is God, have purposed to teach, according to the Scriptures, this doctrine, that the Father, and the Son, and the Holy Spirit intimate a divine unity of one and the same substance in an indivisible equality; and therefore that they are not three Gods, but one God: although the Father hath begotten the Son, and so He who is the Son is not the Father; and the Holy Spirit is neither the Father nor the Son, but only the Spirit of the Father and of the Son, Himself also co-equal with the Father and the Son, and pertaining to the unity of the Trinity. *On the Trinity* 1.4.

3. Christ as God is superior to humanity.

234. Therefore the apostle does not say, "There is one Mediator between God and men, even Jesus Christ;" but his words are, "The MAN Christ Jesus." He is the Mediator, then, in that He is man,— inferior to the Father, by so much as He is nearer to ourselves, and superior to us, by so much as He is nearer to the Father. This is more openly expressed thus: "He is inferior to the Father, because in the form of a servant;" superior to us, because without spot of sin. *On Original Sin* 33.

4. Christ's divinity cannot be seen by human eyes.

235. But perhaps what follows may interfere with this meaning; because it is said, "Whom no man hath seen, nor can see:" although this may also be taken as belonging to Christ according to His divinity, which the Jews did not see, who yet saw and crucified Him in the flesh; whereas His divinity can in no wise be seen by human sight, but is seen with that sight with which they who see are no longer men, but beyond men. *On the Trinity* 1.6.

236. Hence also is that which is said, "If ye loved me, ye would rejoice because I said, "I go unto the Father; for my Father is greater than I:" that is, on that account it is necessary for me to go to the Father, because, whilst you see me thus, you hold me to be less than the Father through that which you see; and so, being taken up with the creature and the "fashion" which I have taken upon me, you do not perceive the equality which I have with the Father. Hence, too, is this: "Touch me not; for I am not yet ascended to my Father." For touch, as it were, puts a limit to their conception, and He therefore would not have the thought of the heart, directed towards Himself, to be so limited as that He should be held to be only that which He seemed to be. *On the Trinity* 1.9.

B. Christ as God is inseparable from the Father.

237. As the Father and the Son are inseparable, so also the works of the Father and of the Son are inseparable. How are the Father and the Son inseparable, since He Himself said, "I and the Father are one"? Because the Father and the Son are not two Gods, but one God, the Word and He whose the Word is, One and the Only One, Father and Son bound together by charity, One God, and the Spirit of Charity also one, so that Father, Son, and Holy Spirit is made the Trinity. Therefore, not only of the Father and Son, but also of the Holy Spirit; as there is equality and inseparability of persons, so also the works are inseparable. *On the Gospel of John* 20.3.

1. Christ and the Father are the same substance and nature.

238. But herein is declared, not only that He is God, but also that He is of the same substance with the Father; because, after saying, "And

the Word was God," it is said also, "The same was in the beginning
with God: all things were made by Him, and without Him was not
anything made." Not simply "all things;" but only all things that were
made, that is, the whole creature; but if He is not a creature, then He
is of the same substance with the Father. For all substance that is not
God is creature; and all that is not creature is God. *On the Trinity* 1.6.

239. Father is Father, Son is Son. Thou sayest now, Father is Father,
Son is Son: thou hast fortunately escaped the danger of the absorbing
whirl; why wouldst thou go unto the other side to say, the Father is
this, the Son that? The Son is another person than the Father is, this
thou sayest rightly; but that He is different in nature, thou sayest not
rightly. Certainly the Son is another person, because He is not the
same who is Father; and the Father is another person, because He is
not the same who is Son: nevertheless, they are not different in
nature, but the selfsame is both Father and Son. *On the Gospel of
John* 36.9.

2. Christ existed eternally with the Father.

240. God Almighty, His only Son our Lord; of that am I first speaking.
Do not imagine in this Nativity a beginning of time; do not imagine
any space of eternity in which the Father was and the Son was not.
Since when the Father was, since then the Son. And what is that
"since," where is no beginning? Therefore ever Father without
beginning, ever Son without beginning. And how, thou wilt say, was
He begotten, if He have no beginning? Of eternal, co-eternal. At no
time was the Father, and the Son not, and yet Son of Father was
begotten. *On the Creed* 8.

241. But assuredly it was in that Word of God itself which was in the
beginning with God and was God, namely, in the wisdom itself of
God, apart from time, at what time that wisdom must needs appear
in the flesh. Therefore, since without any commencement of time,
the Word was in the beginning, and the Word was with God, and the
Word was God, it was in the Word itself without any time, at what
time the Word was to be made flesh and dwell among us. *On the
Trinity* 2.5.

3. Christ's eternal existence with the Father was not
   as a man.

242. For if the apostle has said of us, "According as He hath chosen
us in Him before the foundation of the world," why should it be
thought incongruous with the truth, if the Father glorified our Head
at the same time as He chose us in Him to be His members? For we
were chosen in the same way as He was glorified; inasmuch as
before the world was, neither we nor the Mediator between God and
men, the *man* Christ Jesus, were yet in existence. *On the Gospel of
John* 105.7.

4. Christ has perfect equality with God.

243. What then shall we say, if any one say, "The Father then is to
the Son, such as the brightness is to the fire, and the image to the
shrub"? See I have understood the Father to be eternal; and the Son
to be co-eternal with Him; nevertheless say we that He is as the
brightness which is thrown out from and is less brilliant than the
fire, or as the image which is reflected from and has less real existence than the shrub? No, but there is a thorough equality. "I do not
believe it," he will say, "because thou hast not discovered a resemblance." Well then, believe the Apostle, because he was able to see
what I have said. For he says, "He thought it not robbery to be equal
with God." Equality is perfect likeness in every way. And what said
he? "Not robbery." Why? Because that is robbery which belongs to
another. *Sermons on New Testament Lessons* 67.13.

5. Christ as God is a "pure emanation" from the Father.

244. What wonder, therefore, if He is sent, not because He is unequal
with the Father, but because He is a "pure emanation [*manatio*]
issuing from the glory of the Almighty God?" For there, that which
issues and that from which it issues, is of one and the same substance. *On the Trinity* 4.20.

6. Christ is begotten of the Father.

245. Do not imagine an Almighty Father and a not Almighty Son: it
is error, blot it out within you, let it not cleave in your memory, let it
not be drunk into your faith, and if haply any of you shall have

drunk it in let him vomit it up. Almighty is the Father, Almighty the Son. If Almighty begat not Almighty, He begat not very Son. For what say we, brethren, if the Father being greater begat a Son less than He? What said I, begat? Man engenders, being greater, a son being less: it is true: but that is because the one grows old, the other grows up, and by very growing attains to the form of his father. The Son of God, if He groweth not because neither can God wax old, was begotten perfect. And being begotten perfect, if He groweth not, and remained not less, He is equal. For that ye may know Almighty begotten of Almighty, hear Him Who is Truth. *On the Creed* 5.

C. Christ's actions are as God's.

1. Christ as God created the world.

246. But was not either the Father or the Son "borne over the waters?" If we understand this to mean in space, as a body, then neither was the Holy Spirit; but if the incommutable super-eminence of Divinity above everything mutable, then both Father, and Son, and Holy Ghost were borne "over the waters." *Confessions* 13.9.

2. Christ as God performed miracles in the Old Testament.

247. And the Lord said to them, "In this rejoice not, that the devils are subject unto you; rejoice rather, because your names are written in heaven." To whom He would, He gave the power to cast out devils, to whom He would, He gave the power to raise the dead. Such miracles were done even before the Incarnation of the Lord; the dead were raised, lepers were cleansed; we read of these things. And who did them then, but He who in after time was the Man-Christ after David, but God-Christ before Abraham? He gave the power for all these things, He did them Himself by men; yet gave He not that power to all. *Sermons on New Testament Lessons* 92.7.

3. Christ as God willed His birth by a virgin.

248. The being born, ye have; but also the growing, ye ought to have; because no man begins with being perfect. As for the Son of God, indeed, He could be born perfect, because He was begotten without time, coeternal with the Father, long before all things, not in age, but in eternity. He then was begotten coeternal, of which genera-tion the Prophet said, "His generation who shall declare?" begotten of the Father without time, He was born of the Virgin in the fullness of times. This nativity had times going before it. In opportunity of time, when He would, when He knew, then was He born: for He was not born without His will. None of us is born because he will, and none of us dies when he will: He, when He would, was born; when He would, He died: how He would, He was born of a Virgin; how He would, He died; on the cross. Whatever He would, He did: because He was in such wise Man that, unseen, He was God; God assuming, Man assumed; One Christ, God and Man. *On the Creed* 8.

4. Christ as God performed the miracle of the virgin birth.

249. Lo, in this very Birth, there are at once two things, one which thou mayest see, and another thou mayest not see; but so that by this which thou seest, thou mayest believe that which thou seest not. Thou hadst begun to despise, because thou seest Him who was born; believe what thou dost not see, that He was born of a virgin. "How trifling a person," says one, "is he who was born!" And He who was born of a virgin brought thee a temporal miracle; He was not born of a father, of any man, I mean, His father, yet was He born of the flesh. But let it not seem impossible to thee, that He was born by His mother only, Who made man before father and mother.

He brought thee then a temporal miracle, that thou mayest seek and admire Him who is Eternal. For He "who came forth as a Bride-groom out of His chamber," that is, out of the virgin's womb, where the holy nuptials were celebrated of the Word and the Flesh: He brought, I say, a temporal miracle; but He is Himself eternal, He is co-eternal with the Father, He it is, who "In the beginning was the Word, and the Word was with God, and the Word was God." *Sermons on New Testament Lessons* 76.5,6.

5. Christ as God anointed Himself as the Son of God.

250. For thus behoved it that He should be born as Man, albeit He was ever God, by which birth He might become a God unto us. Hence again the Prophet says concerning Him, "Thy Throne, O God, is for ever and ever; a sceptre of right, the sceptre of Thy Kingdom. Thou has loved righteousness, and hated iniquity; therefore God, Thy God, hath anointed Thee with the oil of gladness above Thy fellows." This anointing is spiritual, wherewith God anointed God, the Father, that is, the Son: whence called from the "Chrism," that is, from the anointing, we know Him as Christ. *Concerning Faith of Things Not Seen* 5.

6. Christ as God raised Himself from the dead.

251. He who was raised and exalted is the Lord. Who raised Him? The Father, to whom He said in the psalms, "Raise me up and I will requite them." Hence, the Father raised Him up. Did He not raise Himself? And doeth the Father anything without the Word? What doeth the Father without His only One? For, hear that He also was God. "Destroy this temple, and in three days I will raise it up." Did He say, Destroy the temple, which in three days the Father will raise up? But as when the Father raiseth, the Son also raiseth; so when the Son raiseth, the Father also raiseth: because the Son has said, "I and the Father are one." *On the Gospel of John* 10.11.

D. *Christ as God is the Mediator for men with God.*

252. And that in this faith it might advance the more confidently towards the truth, the truth itself, God, God's Son, assuming humanity without destroying His divinity, established and founded this faith, that there might be a way for man to man's God through a God-man. For this is the Mediator between God and men, the man Christ Jesus. For it is as man that He is the Mediator and the Way. Since, if the way lieth between him who goes, and the place whither he goes, there is hope of his reaching it; but if there be no way, or if he know not where it is, what boots it to know whither he should go? Now the only way that is infallibly secured against all mistakes, is when the very same person is at once God and man, God our end, man our say. *City of God* 11.2.

III. Humanity and Deity: Christ as God and man united in one person

A. *Christ incarnate is simultaneously human and divine.*

253. Christ, therefore, is one; the Word, soul and flesh, one Christ; the Son of God and Son of man, one Christ; Son of God always, Son of man in time, yet one Christ in regard to unity of person. In heaven He was when He spoke on earth. He was Son of man in heaven in that manner in which He was Son of God on earth; Son of God on earth in the flesh which He took, Son of man in heaven in the unity of person. *On the Gospel of John* 27.4.

254. Moreover, His mercy and grace, published to men by Christ, who is Himself man, and imparted to man by the same Christ, who is also God and the Son of God, never fail those who live by faith in Him and piously worship Him, in adversity patiently and bravely bearing self-control and with compassion for others the good things of this life. *Letters* 137.20.

     1. Christ was coequal with the Father
        before the incarnation.

255. But assuredly it was in that Word of God itself which was in the beginning with God and was God, namely, in the wisdom itself of God, apart from time, at what time that wisdom must needs appear in the flesh. *On the Trinity* 2.5.

     2. Christ was coequal with the Father after the incarnation.

256. And, accordingly, He was both made less and remained equal, being both in one, as has been said: but He was one of these as Word, and the other as man. As Word, He is equal with the Father; as man, less than the Father. One Son of God, and at the same time Son of man; one Son of man, and at the same time Son of God: God without beginning; man with a beginning, our Lord Jesus Christ. *Enchiridion* 35.

B. *Christ has both "form of God" and "form of servant."*

257. They say, for instance, that the Son is less than the Father, because it is written that the Lord Himself said, "My Father is greater than I." But the truth shows that after the same sense the Son is less also than Himself; for how was He not made less also than Himself, who "emptied Himself, and took upon Him the form of a servant?" For He did not so take the form of a servant as that He should lose the form of God, in which He was equal to the Father. If, then, the form of a servant was so taken that the form of God was not lost, since both in the form of a servant and in the form of God He Himself is the same only-begotten Son of God the Father, in the form of God equal to the Father, in the form of a servant the Mediator between God and men, the man Christ Jesus; is there any one who cannot perceive that He Himself in the form of God is also greater than Himself, but yet likewise in the form of a servant less than Himself? *On the Trinity* 1.7.

1. Christ exists in the "form of God."

258. He became the Son of man; and He Himself unites both natures in His own identity, and both natures constitute one Christ; because, "being in the form of God, He thought it not robbery to be," what He was by nature, "equal with God." But He made Himself of no reputation, and took upon Himself the form of a servant, not losing or lessening the form of God. *Enchiridion* 35.

2. Christ's divine nature did not become human or vice versa (see also 240–242).

259. Therefore, because the form of God took the form of a servant, both is God and both is man; but both God, on account of God who takes; and both man, on account of man who is taken. For neither by that taking is the one of them turned and changed into the other: the Divinity is not changed into the creature, so as to cease to be Divinity; nor the creature into Divinity, so as to cease to be creature. *On the Trinity* 1.7.

3. Christ's eternal nature did not become temporal in His incarnation.

260. What, then, is the soul itself which is beyond the bodily senses, that is to say, which resides in the understanding whereby it considers these mysteries? For it is not by means of the senses themselves. And do we suppose that something incredible is told us regarding the omnipotence of God, when it is affirmed that the Word of God, by whom all things were made, did so assume a body from the Virgin, and manifest Himself with mortal senses, as neither to destroy His own immortality, nor to change His eternity, nor to diminish His power, nor to relinquish the government of the world, nor to withdraw from the bosom of the Father, that is, from the secret place where He is with Him and in Him?

Understand the nature of the Word of God, by whom all things were made, to be such that you cannot think of any part of the Word as passing, and, from being future, becoming past. He remains as He is, and He is everywhere in His entirety. He comes when He is manifested, and departs when He is concealed. But whether concealed or manifested, He is present with us as light is present to the eyes both of the seeing and of the blind; but it is felt to be present by the man who sees, and absent by him who is blind. *Letters* 137.2.

261. Wherefore the Word of God, who is also the Son of God, co-eternal with the Father, the Power and the Wisdom of God, mightily pervading and harmoniously ordering all things, from the highest limit of the intelligent to the lowest limit of the material creation, revealed and concealed, nowhere confined, nowhere divided, nowhere distended, but without dimensions, everywhere present in His entirety,—this Word of God, I say, took to Himself, in a manner entirely different from that in which He is present to other creatures, the soul and body of a man, and made, by the union of Himself therewith, the one person Jesus Christ, Mediator between God and men, in His Deity equal with the Father, in His flesh, i.e. in His human nature, inferior to the Father,—unchangeably immortal in respect of the divine nature, in which He is equal with the Father, and yet changeable and mortal in respect of the infirmity which was His through participation with our nature. *Letters* 137.3.

> 4. Christ's human nature is completely different
> from His divine nature.

262. Some insist upon being furnished with an explanation of the manner in which the Godhead was so united with a human soul and body as to constitute the one person of Christ, when it was necessary that this should be done once in the world's history, with as much boldness as if they were themselves able to furnish an explanation of the manner in which the soul is so united to the body as to constitute the one person of a man, an event which is occurring every day. For just as the soul is united to the body in one person so as to constitute man, in the same way is God united to man in one person so as to constitute Christ. In the former personality there is a combination of soul and body; in the latter there is a combination of the Godhead and man. Let my reader, however, guard against borrowing his idea of the combination from the properties of material bodies, by which two fluids when combined are so mixed that neither preserves its original character; although even among material bodies there are exceptions, such as light, which sustains no change when combined with the atmosphere. In the person of man, therefore, there is a combination of soul and body; in the person of Christ there is a combination of the Godhead with man; for when the Word of God was united to a soul having a body, He took into union with Himself both the soul and the body. *Letters* 137.3.

5. Both natures of Christ are united in one person.

263. In the body which thus became His, He who, without any liability to change in Himself, has woven according to His counsel the vicissitudes of all past centuries, became subject to the succession of seasons and the ordinary stages of the life of man. For His body, as it began to exist at a point of time, became developed with the lapse of time. But the Word of God, who was in the beginning, and to whom the ages of time owe their existence, did not bow to time as bringing round the event of His incarnation apart from His consent, but chose the point of time at which He freely took our nature to Himself. The human nature was brought into union with the divine; God did not withdraw from Himself. *Letters* 137.3.

264. Wherefore Christ Jesus, the Son of God, is both God and man; God before all worlds; man in our world: God, because the Word of God (for "the Word was God"); and man, because in His one person the Word was joined with a body and a rational soul. *Enchiridion* 35.

a) The union is like that of soul and body.

265. For just as the soul is united to the body in one person so as to constitute man, in the same way is God united to man in one person so as to constitute Christ. In the former personality there is a combination of soul and body; in the latter there is a combination of the Godhead and man. *Letters* 137.3.

b) The union does not reduce God to a bodily location.

266. In the first place, I wish you to understand that the Christian doctrine does not hold that the Godhead was so blended with the human nature in which He was born of the virgin that He either relinquished or lost the administration of the universe, or transferred it to that body as a small and limited material substance. *Letters* 137.2.

c) The union does not separate Christ from the Father.

267. How much more do they err if they compare them with Christ, of whom the prophets, so incomparably superior to magicians of every name, foretold that He would come both in the human nature, which he took in being born of the Virgin, and in the divine nature, in which He is never separated from the Father! *Letters* 138.4.

d) The union does not pollute Christ's divine nature.

268. Far be it from the incontaminable God to fear pollution from the man He assumed, or from the men among whom He lived in the form of a man. For, though His incarnation showed us nothing else, these two wholesome facts were enough, that true divinity cannot be polluted by flesh, and that demons are not to be considered better than ourselves because they have not flesh. *City of God* 9.17.

C. Christ as the Word (logos) is begotten of the Father.

1. The eternal Word is unchangeable.

269. This Word, however, we ought not to apprehend merely in the sense in which we think of our own words, which are given forth by the voice and the mouth, and strike the air and pass on, and subsist no longer than their sound continues. For that Word remains unchangeably: for of this very Word was it spoken when of Wisdom it was said, "Remaining in herself, she maketh all things new." Moreover, the reason of His being named the Word of the Father, is that the Father is made known by Him. Accordingly, just as it is our intention, when we speak truth, that by means of our words our mind should be made known to him who hears us, and that whatever we carry in secrecy in our heart may be set forth by means of signs of this sort for the intelligent understanding of another individual; so this Wisdom that God the Father begat is most appropriately named His Word, inasmuch as the most hidden Father is made known to worthy minds by the same. *On Faith and the Creed* 3.

2. The eternal Word is the same substance as the Father.

270. Among the many things which the Arians are wont to dispute against the Catholic faith, they seem chiefly to set forth this, as their most crafty device, namely, that whatsoever is said or understood of God, is said not according to accident, but according to substance: and therefore, to be unbegotten belongs to the Father according to substance, and to be begotten belongs to the Son according to substance; but to be unbegotten and to be begotten are different; therefore the substance of the Father and that of the Son are different. To whom we reply, If whatever is spoken of God is spoken according to substance, then that which is said, "I and the Father are one," is spoken according to substance. Therefore there is one substance of the Father and the Son. *On the Trinity* 5.3.

3. The Word is eternally begotten of the Father.

271. Wherefore let him who can understand the generation of the Son from the Father without time, understand also the procession of the Holy Spirit from both without time. And let him who can understand, in that which the Son says, "As the Father hath life in Himself, so hath He given to the Son to have life in Himself," not that the Father gave life to the Son already existing without life, but that He so begat Him apart from time, that the life which the Father gave to the Son by begetting Him is co-eternal with the life of the Father who gave it: let him, I say, understand, that as the Father has in Himself that the Holy Spirit should proceed from Him, so has He given to the Son that the same Holy Spirit should proceed from Him, and be both apart from time: and that the Holy Spirit is so said to proceed from the Father as that it be understood that His proceeding also from the Son, is a property derived by the Son from the Father. *On the Trinity* 15.26.

4. The Word is *of* God, not *from* God.

272. But "from Him" does not mean the same as "of Him." For what is of Him may be said to be from Him; but not everything that is from Him is rightly said to be of Him. For from Him are heaven and earth, because He made them; but not of Him because they are not of His substance. As in the case of a man who begets a son and makes a house, from himself is the son, from himself is the house, but the son is of him, the house is of earth and wood. But this is so, because as a man he cannot make something even of nothing; but God of whom are all things, through whom are all things, in whom are all things, had no need of any material which He had not made to assist His omnipotence. *On the Nature of Good* 27.

D. Christ as man and God exists in both time and eternity (see also 240-242, 259-261).

    1. Christ's eternal nature did not become temporal in the incarnation.

273. And do we suppose that something incredible is told us regarding the omnipotence of God, when it is affirmed that the Word of God, by whom all things were made, did so assume a body from the Virgin, and manifest Himself with mortal senses, as neither to destroy His own immortality, nor to change His eternity, nor to diminish His power, nor to relinquish the government of the world, nor to withdraw from the bosom of the Father, that is, from the secret place where He is with Him and in Him?

Understand the nature of the Word of God, by whom all things were made, to be such that you cannot think of any part of the Word as passing, and, from being future, becoming past. He remains as He is, and He is everywhere in His entirety. He comes when He is manifested, and departs when He is concealed. *Letters* 137.2.

    2. Christ's human nature is entirely different from His divine nature.

274. Wherefore the Word of God, who is also the Son of God, co-eternal with the Father, the Power and the Wisdom of God, mightily pervading and harmoniously ordering all things, from the highest limit of the intelligent to the lowest limit of the material creation, revealed and concealed, nowhere confined, nowhere divided, nowhere distended, but without dimensions, everywhere present in His entirety,—this Word of God, I say, took to Himself, in a manner entirely different from that in which He is present to other creatures, the soul and body of a man, and made, by the union of Himself therewith, the one person Jesus Christ, Mediator between God and men, in His Deity equal with the Father, in His flesh, i.e. in His human nature, inferior to the Father,—unchangeably immortal in respect of the divine nature, in which He is equal with the Father, and yet changeable and mortal in respect of the infirmity which was His through participation with our nature. *Letters* 137.3.

3. One nature is temporal and the other is eternal.

275. In the body which thus became His, He who, without any liability to change in Himself, has woven according to His counsel the vicissitudes of all past centuries, became subject to the succession of seasons and the ordinary stages of the life of man. For His body, as it began to exist at a point of time, became developed with the lapse of time. But the Word of God, who was in the beginning, and to whom the ages of time owe their existence, did not bow to time as bringing round the event of His incarnation apart from His consent, but chose the point of time at which He freely took our nature to Himself. The human nature was brought into union with the divine; God did not withdraw from Himself. *Letters* 137.3.

4. Both natures are united in one person.

276. Some insist upon being furnished with an explanation of the manner in which the Godhead was so united with a human soul and body as to constitute the one person of Christ, when it was necessary that this should be done once in the world's history, with as much boldness as if they were themselves able to furnish an explanation of the manner in which the soul is so united to the body as to constitute the one person of a man, an event which is occurring every day. For just as the soul is united to the body in one person so as to constitute man, in the same way is God united to man in one person so as to constitute Christ. In the former personality there is a combination of soul and body; in the latter there is a combination of the Godhead and man. Let my reader, however, guard against borrowing his idea of the combination from the properties of material bodies, by which two fluids when combined are so mixed that neither preserves its original character. *Letters* 137.3.

5

Man

I. The creation of man

A. Man was created by God.

277. Great art Thou, O Lord, and greatly to be praised; great is Thy power, and of Thy wisdom there is no end. And man, being a part of Thy creation, desires to praise Thee—man, who bears about with him his mortality, the witness of his sin, even the witness that Thou "resistest the proud"—yet man, this part of Thy creation, desires to praise Thee. *Confessions* 1.1.

278. Thou, therefore, O Lord my God, who gavest life to the infant, and a frame which, as we see, Thou hast endowed with senses, compacted with limbs, beautiful with form, and, for its general good and safety, hast introduced all vital energies—Thou commandest me to praise Thee for these things, "to give thanks unto the Lord, and to sing praise unto Thy name, O Most High;" for Thou art a God omnipotent and good, though Thou hadst done nought but these things, O Thou most fair, who madest all things fair, and orderest all according to thy law. *Confessions* 1.7.

279. The Apostle Paul certainly uses the expression *the inner man* for the spirit of the mind, and *the outer man* for the body and for this mortal life; but we nowhere find him making these two different men, but one, which is all made by God, both the inner and the outer. *Reply to Faustus the Manichaean* 24.2.

280. Therefore God supreme and true, with His Word and Holy Spirit (which three are one), one God omnipotent, creator and maker of every soul and of every body; by whose gift all are happy who are happy through verity and not through vanity; who made man a rational animal consisting of soul and body, . . . from whom is everything which has an existence in nature, of whatever kind it be, and of whatever value; from whom are the seeds of forms and the forms of seeds, and the motion of seeds and of forms; who gave also to flesh its origin, beauty, health, reproductive fecundity, disposition of members, and the salutary concord of its parts; who also to the irrational soul has given memory, sense, appetite, but to the rational soul, in addition to these, has given intelligence and will. . . . *City of God* 5.11.

1. Man was created sinless.

281. Man's nature, indeed, was created at first faultless and without any sin; but that nature of man in which every one is born from Adam, now wants the Physician, because it is not sound. *On Nature and Grace* 3.

282. It is He who made also himself upright, with the same freedom of will—an earthly animal, indeed, but fit for heaven if he remained faithful to his Creator, but destined to the misery appropriate to such a nature if he forsook Him. *City of God* 22.1.

283. But by nature, as God first created us, no one is the slave either of man or of sin. *City of God* 19.15.

2. Adam was created *ex nihilo.*

284. Far be it, however, from us to say, that the Almighty could not have made the breath of life out of nothing, by which man might become a living soul; and to crowd ourselves into such straits, as that we must either think that something already existed other than Himself, out of which He formed breath, or else suppose that He formed out of Himself that which we see was made subject to change. Now, whatever is out of Himself, and therefore immutable: but the soul (as all allow) is mutable. Therefore it is not out of Him, because it is not immutable, as He is. If, however, it was not made of anything else; it was undoubtedly made out of nothing—but by Himself. *On the Soul and Its Origin* 1.4.

285. For though God formed man of the dust of the earth, yet the earth itself, and every earthly material, is absolutely created out of nothing; and man's soul, too, God created out of nothing, and joined to the body, when He made man. *City of God* 14.11.

3. The human race is unified in Adam.

286. And therefore God created only one single man, not, certainly, that he might be a solitary, bereft of all society, but that by this means the unity of society and the bond of concord might be more effectually commended to him, men being bound together not only by similarity of nature, but by family affection. And indeed He did not even create woman that was to be given him as his wife, as he created the man, but created her out of the man, that the whole human race might derive from one man. *City of God* 12.21.

287. For from one man, whom God created as the first, the whole human race descended according to the faith of Holy Scripture, which deservedly is of wonderful authority among all nations throughout the world; since, among its other true statements, it predicted, by its divine foresight, that all nations would give credit to it. *City of God* 12.9.

4. Everything God made is good.

288. Accordingly we say that there is no unchangeable good but the one, true, blessed God; that the things which He made are indeed good because from Him, yet mutable because made not out of Him, but out of nothing. *City of God* 12.1.

289. And that no one should perchance suppose that the creator of sex despised sex, he became a man born of a woman. *Of True Religion* 16. TR

B. Man is made in God's image.

290. For Thou, O most high and most near, most secret, yet most present, who hast not limbs some larger some smaller, but art wholly everywhere, and nowhere in space, nor art Thou of such corporeal form, yet hast Thou created man after Thine own image, and, behold, from head to foot is he confined by space. *Confessions* 6.3.

291. It is from the one true and supremely good God that we have that nature in which we are made in the image of God. *City of God* 8.10.

292. Where, then, is the trinity? Let us attend as much as we can, and let us invoke the everlasting light, that He may illuminate our darkness, and that we may see in ourselves, as much as we are permitted, the image of God. *On the Trinity* 9.2.

    1. The *imago dei* is in the soul, or inner man.

293. For a great thing truly is man, made after the image and similitude of God, not as respects the mortal body in which he is clothed, but as respects the rational soul by which he is exalted in honor above the beasts. *On Christian Doctrine* 1.22.

294. For I do not travel very far for examples, when I mean to give thee some similitude to thy God from thy own mind; because surely not in the body, but in that same mind, was man made after the image of God. *On the Gospel of John* 23.10.

295. He made also man after His own image and likeness, in the mind: for in that it is the image of God. This is the reason why the mind cannot be comprehended even by itself, because in it is the image of God. *On the Creed* 2.

296. But, as even you yourself with perfect propriety confess, God is not a body. How, then, could a body receive His image? *On the Soul and Its Origin* 4.20.

    2. The *imago dei* is not wholly blotted out in fallen man.

297. Still, since God's image has not been so completely erased in the soul of man by the stain of earthly affections, as to have left remaining there not even the merest lineaments of it whence it might be justly said that man, even in the ungodliness of his life, does, or appreciates, some things contained in the law; if this is what is meant by the statement that "the Gentiles, which have not the law" (that is, the law of God), "do by nature the things contained in the law," and that men of this character "are a law to themselves," and "show the work of the law written in their hearts"—that is to say, what was impressed on their hearts when they were created in the image of God has not been wholly blotted out:—even in this view of the subject, that wide difference will not be disturbed, which separates the new covenant from the old, and which lies in the fact that by the new covenant the law of God is written in the hearts of believers, whereas in the old it was inscribed on tables of stone. For this writing in the heart is effected by renovation, although it had not been completely blotted out by the old nature. *On the Spirit and the Letter* 48.

3. The *imago dei* reflects the Trinity.

298. For so, too, we find a trinity in man also, i.e. mind, and the knowledge wherewith mind knows itself, and the love wherewith it loves itself. *On the Trinity* 15.6.

299. And we indeed recognize in ourselves the image of God, that is, of the supreme Trinity, an image which, though it be not equal to God, or rather, though it be very far removed from Him—being neither co-eternal, nor, to say all in a word, consubstantial with Him—is yet nearer to Him in nature than any other of His works, and is destined to be yet restored, that it may bear a still closer resemblance. For we both are, and know that we are, and delight in our being, and our knowledge of it. *City of God* 11.26.

300. But that Trinity of which he is the image is nothing else in its totality than God, is nothing else in its totality than the Trinity. Nor does anything pertain to the nature of God so as not to pertain to that Trinity; and the Three Persons are of one essence, not as each individual man is one person. *On the Trinity* 15.7.

4. Even in the fetal stage man reflects the image of God.

301. Hence in the first place arises a question about abortive conceptions, which have indeed been born in the mother's womb, but not so born that they could be born again. For if we shall decide that these are to rise again, we cannot object to any conclusion that may be drawn in regard to those which are fully formed. Now who is there that is not rather disposed to think that unformed abortions perish, like seeds that have never fructified? But who will dare to deny, though he may not dare to affirm, that at the resurrection every defect in the form shall be supplied, and that thus the perfection which time would have brought shall not be wanting, any more than the blemishes which time did bring shall be present; so that the nature shall neither want anything suitable and in harmony with it that length of days would have added, nor be debased by the presence of anything of an opposite kind that length of days have added; but that what is not yet complete shall be completed, just as what has been injured shall be renewed. *Enchiridion* 85.

302. And therefore the following question may be very carefully inquired into and discussed by learned men, though I do not know whether it is in man's power to resolve it: At what time the infant begins to live in the womb: whether life exists in a latent form before it manifests itself in the motions of the living being. To deny that the young who are cut out limb by limb from the womb, lest if they were left there dead the mother should die too, have never been alive, seems too audacious. Now, from the time that a man begins to live, from that time it is possible for him to die. And if he die, wheresoever death may overtake him, I cannot discover on what principle he can be denied an interest in the resurrection of the dead. *Enchiridion* 86.

C. God has created man to have dominion over the animals.

303. And certainly man, even sinful man, is better than a beast. *On the Catechising of the Uninstructed* 18.30.

304. [God] did not intend that His rational creature, who was made in His image, should have dominion over anything but the irrational creation—not man over man, but man over the beasts. And hence the righteous men in primitive times were made shepherds of cattle rather than kings of men, God intending thus to teach us what the relative position of the creatures is, and what the desert of sin; for it is with justice, we believe, that the condition of slavery is the result of sin. *City of God* 19.15.

D. Whether the soul is originated through creation or by propagation is yet to be decided.

305. As for the opinion, that new souls are created by inbreathing without being propagated, we certainly do not in the least object to its maintenance—only let it be by persons who have succeeded in discovering some new evidence, either in the canonical Scriptures, in the shape of unambiguous testimony towards the solution of a most knotty question, or else in their own reasonings, such as shall not be opposed to catholic truth, but not by such persons as this man has shown himself to be. If the doctrine of the propagation of souls is false, may its refutation not be the work of such disputants; and may the defence of the rival principle of the insufflation of new souls in every creative act, proceed from better hands. *On the Soul and Its Origin* 1.33.

306. What shall I say, moreover, as to the [difficulty which besets the theory of the creation of each soul separately at the birth of the individual in connection with the] diversity of talent in different souls, and especially the absolute privation of reason in some? This is, indeed, not apparent in the first stages of infancy, but being developed continuously from the beginning of life, it becomes manifest in children, of whom some are so slow and defective in memory that they cannot learn even the letters of the alphabet, and some (commonly called idiots) so imbecile that they differ very little from the beasts of the field. Perhaps I am told, in answer to this, that the bodies are the cause of these imperfections. *Letters* 166.6.

307. Well, but "if the soul is not propagated, but the flesh alone, then the latter alone has propagation of sin, and it alone deserves punishment:" this is what they think, saying "that it is unjust that the soul which is only recently produced, and that not out of Adam's substance, should bear the sin of another committed so long ago." Now observe, I pray you, how the circumspect Pelagius felt the question about the soul to be a very difficult one, and acted accordingly,—for the words which I have just quoted are copied from his book. He does not say absolutely, "Because the soul is not propagated," but hypothetically, *If the soul is not propagated,* rightly determining on so obscure a subject (on which we can find in Holy Scriptures no certain and obvious testimonies, or with very great difficulty discover any) to speak with hesitation rather than with confidence. *On Forgiveness of Sins, and Baptism* 3.18.

308. God, then, so created man that He gave him what we may call fertility, whereby he might propagate other men, giving them a congenital capacity to propagate their kind, but not imposing on them any necessity to do so. . . . But if conformation were not added to propagation, there would be no reproduction of one's kind. For even though there were no such thing as copulation, and God wished to fill the earth with human inhabitants, He might create all these as He created one without the help of human generation. And, indeed, even as it is, those who copulate can generate nothing save by the creative energy of God. *City of God* 22.24.

E. Man is meant to be in subjection to God.

309. For though the soul may seem to rule the body admirably, and the reason the vices, if the soul and reason do not themselves obey God, as God has commanded them to serve Him, they have no proper authority over the body and the vices. For what kind of mistress of the body and the vices can that mind be which is ignorant of the true God, and which, instead of being subject to His authority, is prostituted to the corrupting influences of the most vicious demons? *City of God* 19.25.

310. And justice, whose office it is to render to every man his due, whereby there is in man himself a certain just order of nature, so that the soul is subjected to God, and the flesh to the soul, and consequently both soul and flesh to God—does not this virtue demonstrate that it is as yet rather laboring towards its end than resting in its finished work? For the soul is so much the less subjected to God as it is less occupied with the thought of God; and the flesh is so much the less subjected to the spirit as it lusts more vehemently against the spirit. *City of God* 19.4.

F. Man's happiness depends on God.

311. Although, therefore, they are not the supreme good, for God is a greater good, yet those mutable things which can adhere to the immutable good, and so be blessed, are very good; for so completely is He their good, that without Him they cannot but be wretched. *City of God* 12.1.

312. Thou movest us to delight in praising Thee; for Thou hast formed us for Thyself, and our hearts are restless till they find rest in Thee. *Confessions* 1.1.

313. If any immortal power, then, no matter with what virtue endowed, loves us as himself, he must desire that we find our happiness by submitting ourselves to Him, in submission to whom he himself finds happiness. If he does not worship God, he is wretched, because deprived of God; if he worships God, he cannot wish to be worshipped in God's stead. *City of God* 10.3.

II. The nature of man

A. Man is a composite being: soul and body.

314. We are made up of soul and body. *Of the Morals of the Catholic Church* 4.

315. For a living creature or animal consists of soul and body. *City of God* 9.9.

316. But if, again, we were so to define man as to say, Man is a rational substance consisting of mind and body, then without doubt man has a soul that is not body, and a body that is not soul. *On the Trinity* 15.7.

B. Man possesses a material part: the body.

1. The body is created by God.

317. And the Apostle: "Thou fool, that which thou sowest is not quickened except it die; and that which thou sowest, thou sowest not that body that shall be, but a bare grain, as perchance of wheat, or of some other corn; but God giveth it a body as He would, and to each one of seeds its proper body." If then it be God that builds our bodies as the temple of the Holy Ghost, doubt not that the Holy

Ghost is God. And do not add as it were a third God; because Father and Son and Holy Ghost is One God. So believe ye. *On the Creed* 13.

   2. The body is a revelation of God's goodness
      and providence.

318. Moreover, even in the body, though it dies like that of the beasts, and is in many ways weaker than theirs, what goodness of God, what providence of the great Creator, is apparent! The organs of sense and the rest of the members, are not they so placed, the appearance, and form, and stature of the body as a whole, is it not so fashioned, as to indicate that it was made for the service of a reasonable soul? *City of God* 22.24.

319. I think, that in the creation of the human body God put form before function. After all, function will pass and the time will come when we shall delight solely in the unlibidinous contemplation of one another's beauty, knowing that our joy will be giving glory to the Creator, of whom the Psalmist says: "Thou hast put on praise and beauty." *City of God* 22.24.

   3. The body is our adversary.

320. I carry on a daily war by fastings, oftentimes "bringing my body into subjection," and my pains are expelled by pleasure. For hunger and thirst are in some sort pains; they consume and destroy like unto a fever, unless the medicine of nourishment relieve us. The which, since it is at hand through the comfort we receive of Thy gifts, with which land and water and air serve our infirmity, our calamity is called pleasure. *Confessions* 10.31.

321. And whereas health is the reason of eating and drinking, there joineth itself as an handmaid a perilous delight, which mostly tries to precede it, in order that I may do for her sake what I say I do, or desire to do, for health's sake. Nor have both the same limit; for what is sufficient for health is too little for pleasure. And oftentimes it is doubtful whether it be the necessary care of the body which still asks nourishment, or whether a sensual snare of desire offers its ministry. In this uncertainty does my unhappy soul rejoice, and therein prepares an excuse as a defence, glad that it doth not appear what may be sufficient for the moderation of health, that so under the pretence of health it may conceal the business of pleasure. *Confessions* 10.31.

322. To a great extent we agree with the adversary while we are with him in the way. The body will be entirely whole without lack or weariness; for this corruptible will put on incorruption in its due time and order, when the resurrection of the flesh comes. *Of True Religion* 53. TR

> 4. The physical body will be resurrected.
>
> a) *The resurrection of the just*

323. Now, as to the resurrection of the body—not a resurrection such as some have had, who came back to life for a time and died again, but a resurrection to eternal life, as the body of Christ Himself rose again—I do not see how I can discuss the matter briefly, and at the same time give a satisfactory answer to all the questions that are ordinarily raised about it. Yet that the bodies of all men—both those who have been born and those who shall be born, both those who have died and those who shall die—shall be raised again, no Christian ought to have the shadow of a doubt. *Enchiridion* 84.

324. Nor does the earthly material out of which men's mortal bodies are created ever perish; but though it may crumble into dust and ashes, or be dissolved into vapors and exhalations, though it may be transformed into the substance of other bodies, or dispersed into the elements, though it should become food for beasts or men, and be changed into their flesh, it returns in a moment of time to that human soul which animated it at the first, and which caused it to become man, and to live and grow. *Enchiridion* 88.

> b) *The resurrection of the unjust*

325. Every soul, moreover, which may at any age whatsoever depart from this life without the grace of the Mediator and the sacrament of this grace, departs to future punishment, and shall receive again its own body at the last judgment as a partner in punishment. But if the soul after its natural generation, which was derived from Adam, be regenerated in Christ, it belongs to His fellowship, and shall not only have rest after the death of the body, but also receive again its own as a partner in glory. These are truths concerning the soul which I hold most firmly. *Letters* 166.11.

326. But as for those who, out of the mass of perdition caused by the first man's sin, are not redeemed through the one Mediator between God and man, they too shall rise again, each with his own body, but only to be punished with the devil and his angels. Now, whether they shall rise again with all their diseases and deformities of body, bringing with them the diseased and deformed limbs which they possessed here, it would be labor lost to inquire. *Enchiridion* 92.

5. The resurrected body is free from all corruption.

327. What power of movement such bodies shall possess, I have not the audacity rashly to define, as I have not the ability to conceive. Nevertheless I will say that in any case, both in motion and at rest, they shall be, as in their appearance, seemly; for into that state nothing which is unseemly shall be admitted. One thing is certain, the body shall forthwith be wherever the spirit wills, and the spirit shall will nothing which is unbecoming either to the spirit or to the body. *City of God* 22.30.

328. What shall the body be, when it is in every respect subject to the spirit, from which it shall draw a life so sufficient, as to stand in need of no other nutriment? For it shall no longer be animal, but spiritual, having indeed the substance of flesh, but without any fleshly corruption. *City of God* 22.24.

6. The resurrected body will live immortally.

329. For as, after the resurrection, the body, having become wholly subject to the spirit, will live in perfect peace to all eternity; even in this life we must make it an object to have the carnal habit changed for the better, so that its inordinate affections may not war against the soul. *On Christian Doctrine* 1.24.

7. The body is mortal apart from the soul.

330. But I see I must speak a little more carefully of the nature of death. For although the human soul is truly affirmed to be immortal, yet it also has a certain death of its own. For it is therefore called immortal, because, in a sense, it does not cease to live and to feel; while the body is called mortal, because it can be forsaken of all life, and cannot by itself live at all. The death, then, of the soul takes place when God forsakes it, as the death of the body when the soul forsakes it. *City of God* 13.2.

C. Man possesses immaterial parts.

1. The soul

a) Soul *must first be defined.*

331. If you wish a definition of what the soul is, I have a ready answer. It seems to me to be a certain kind of substance, sharing in reason, fitted to rule the body. *On the Magnitude of Soul* 12.22. FOC

b) *The soul comes from God and has its own substance.*

332. I believe that God, its Creator, is, so to speak, the soul's proper habitation and its home. As for its substance, I really cannot find a name. I certainly do not think that it belongs to those ordinary and familiar things of which we are aware of through senses. I do not think that the soul is composed either of earth or water or air or fire, or of all of these together, or of any combination of them. Just as I cannot deny that earth was made by God and still I cannot say of what other elements, so to speak, earth is composed; for earth lacks parts in so far as it is earth, and for that reason is said to be an element of all those bodies that are formed from the four elements. Therefore, there is no contradiction in my statement that the soul is made by God and has its own proper nature. God Himself is the author of the soul's peculiar nature, just as He is the maker of fire, air, water, and earth—the elements that make up all other things. *On the Magnitude of Soul* 1.2. FOC

333. Whence it is perceived that the soul, whether it be termed material or immaterial, has a certain nature of its own, created from a substance superior to the elements of this world—a substance which cannot be truly conceived of by any representation of the material images perceived by the bodily senses, but which is apprehended by the understanding and discovered to our consciousness by its living energy. These things I am. *Letters* 166.11.

c) *The soul is nonmaterial.*

334. That the soul is immaterial is a fact of which I avow myself to

be fu**   understanding are hard to

understanding of man, the rational soul;
**ot a body, since that similitude of a body which it
**judges of is itself not a body. The soul is neither earth,
n**   **ter, nor fire, of which four bodies, called the four elements, we
see that this world is composed. And if the soul is not a body, how
should God, its Creator, be a body? *City of God* 8.5.

d) The rational soul is higher than other kinds of souls.

336. We worship God—not heaven and earth, of which two parts
this world consists, nor the soul or souls diffused through all living
things—but God who made heaven and earth, and all things which
are in them; who made every soul, whatever be the nature of its life,
whether it have life without sensation and reason, or life with sensation, or life with both sensation and reason. *City of God* 7.29.

e) The soul is liable to corruption.

337. The Manichaeans would not drivel, or rather, rave in such a
style as this, if they believed the nature of God to be, as it is, unchangeable and absolutely incorruptible, and subject to no injury; and if,
moreover, they held in Christian sobriety, that the soul which has
shown itself capable of being altered for the worse by its own will,
and of being corrupted by sin, and so, of being deprived of the light
of eternal truth—that this soul, I say, is not a part of God, nor of the
same nature as God, but is created by Him, and is far different from
its Creator. *City of God* 11.22.

f) The soul is conscious in the intermediate state.

338. Now, in the time intervening between a man's death and the
final resurrection, the soul is held in a hidden retreat, enjoying rest
or suffering hardship in accordance with what it merited during its
life in the body. *Enchiridion* 29.

g) The soul is immortal.

339. I have no doubt either that the soul is immortal—not in the
same sense in which God is immortal, who alone hath immortality,
but in a certain way peculiar to itself—or that the soul is a creature

and not a part of the substance of the Creator, or as to any other thing which I regard as most certain concerning its nature. *Letters* 143.7.

340. That body, indeed, which shall be made spiritual and immortal by the quickening Spirit shall not be able to die at all; as the soul has been created immortal, and therefore, although by sin it may be said to die, and does lose a certain life of its own, namely, the Spirit of God, by whom it was enabled to live wisely and blessedly, yet it does not cease living a kind of life, though a miserable, because it is immortal by creation. *City of God* 13.24.

341. The soul of man is in a sense proper to itself immortal. It is not absolutely immortal, as God is, of whom it is written that He "alone hath immortality," for Holy Scripture makes mention of deaths to which the soul is liable—as in the saying, "Let the dead bury their dead;" but because when alienated from the life of God it so dies as not wholly to cease from living in its own nature, it is found to be from a certain cause mortal, yet so as to be not without reason called at the same time immortal. *Letters* 166.11.

h) The soul needs redemption.

342. The soul sinned, and therefore is miserable. It accepted free choice, used free choice, as it willed; it fell, was cast out from blessedness, was implicated in miseries. *Against Fortunatus* 25.

343. I am, moreover, fully persuaded that the soul has fallen into sin, not through the fault of God, nor through any necessity either in the divine nature or in its own, but by its own free will; and that it can be delivered from the body of this death not by the strength of its own will, as if there were in itself sufficient to achieve. . . . *Letters* 166.11.

i) The soul of glorified man will possess free will.

344. Neither are we to suppose that because sin shall have no power to delight them, free will must be withdrawn. It will, on the contrary, be all the more truly free, because set free from delight in sinning to take unfailing delight in not sinning. In that city, then, there shall be free will, one in all the citizens, and indivisible in each, delivered

from all ill, filled with all good, enjoying indefeasibly the delights of
eternal joys, oblivious of sins, oblivious of sufferings, and yet not so
oblivious of its deliverance as to be ungrateful to its Deliverer. *City of
God* 22.30.

2. The mind

a) The mind has the power of reasoning.

345. It is He, then, who has given to the human soul a mind, in
which reason and understanding lie as it were asleep during infancy,
and if they were not, destined, however, to be awakened and exer-
cised as years increase, so as to become capable of knowledge and
of receiving instruction, fit to understand what is true and to love
what is good. It is by this capacity the soul drinks in wisdom, and
becomes endowed with those virtues by which, in prudence, fortitude, temperance, and righteousness, it makes war upon error and
the other inborn vices, and conquers them by fixing its desires upon
no other object than the supreme and unchangeable Good. And
even though this be not uniformly the result, yet who can compe-
tently utter or even conceive the grandeur of this work of the
Almighty, and the unspeakable boon He has conferred upon our
rational nature, by giving us even the capacity of such attainment?
City of God 22.24.

b) The mind is immortal.

346. But, since there is no place for art without life, so life with
reason belongs to nothing but the mind. Moreover, what exists
cannot be nowhere, nor can what is immutable at any time not exist.
However, if art passes from mind to mind, leaving the one, in order
to dwell in the other, then nobody teaches art without losing it, or,
again, nobody becomes educated but by the forgetting or the death
of his teacher. If these statements are most absurd and false, as they
really are, then the human mind is immortal. *On the Immortality of
the Soul* 4. FOC

347. For we mean by eternal life that life where there is endless
happiness. For if the soul live in eternal punishments, by which also
those unclean spirits shall be tormented, that is rather eternal death
than eternal life. For there is no greater or worse death than when
death never dies. But because the soul from its very nature, being

created immortal, cannot be without some kind of life, its utmost death is alienation from the life of God in an eternity of punishment. *City of God* 6.12.

c) The mind is darkened by sin.

348. But since the mind itself, though naturally capable of reason and intelligence, is disabled by besotting and inveterate vices not merely from delighting and abiding in, but even from tolerating His unchangeable light, until it has been gradually healed, and renewed, and made capable of such felicity, it had, in the first place, to be impregnated with faith, and so purified. *City of God* 11.2.

349. But even in respect of these things, had the mind not been mutable, it would not have been possible for one to judge better than another with regard to sensible forms. He who is clever, judges better than he who is slow, he who is skilled than he who is unskillful, he who is practised than he who is unpractised; and the same person judges better after he has gained experience than he did before. *City of God* 8.6.

3. The will (see especially chapter 7, Free Will and Grace, 473–495)

D. *Material and immaterial are related.*

1. God set spiritual creation above the corporeal.

350. Notwithstanding what I have just said, I am prepared to defend the sentence in the third book of my treatise on *Free Will*, in which, discoursing on the rational substance, I have expressed my opinion in these words: "The soul, appointed to occupy a body inferior in nature to itself after the entrance of sin, governs its own body, not absolutely according to its free will, but only in so far as the laws of the universe permit." *Letters* 143.5.

2. The body is inferior to the soul.

351. This, indeed, is true, that the soul is not the whole man, but the better part of man; the body not the whole, but the inferior part of man; and that then, when both are joined, they receive the name of man—which, however, they do not severally lose even when we speak of them singly. *City of God* 13.24.

352. We must admit that a weeping man is better than a happy worm. *Of True Religion* 12. TR

353. For a living creature or animal consists of soul and body, and of these two parts the soul is undoubtedly the better; even though vicious and weak, it is obviously better than even the soundest and strongest body, for the greater excellence of its nature is not reduced to the level of the body even by the pollution of vice, as gold, even when tarnished, is more precious than the purest silver or lead. *City of God* 9.9.

354. If, then, the body, which, being inferior, the soul uses as a servant or instrument, is a sacrifice when it is used rightly, and with reference to God, how much more does the soul itself become a sacrifice when it offers itself to God, in order that, being inflamed by the fire of His love, it may receive of His beauty and become pleasing to Him, losing the shape of earthly desire, and being remoulded in the image of permanent loveliness? *City of God* 10.6.

3. The body is inferior to the mind.

355. All admit that these things are perceived by the body, and that the mind is better than the body. *Of True Religion* 52. TR

356. For, the mind is certainly better and more alive than the body, since it is the mind that gives life to the body. *On the Immortality of the Soul* 7.

4. The soul gives life and direction to the body.

357. For so long as the soul is in the body, especially if consciousness remain, the man certainly lives; for body and soul constitute the man. And thus, before death, he cannot be said to be in death, but when, on the other hand, the soul has departed, and all bodily sensation is extinct, death is past, and the man is dead. *City of God* 13.11.

5. The soul animates the whole body.

358. The soul is not material. For it pervades the whole body which it animates, not by a local distribution of parts, but by a certain vital influence, being at the same moment present in its entirety in all parts of the body, and not less in smaller parts and greater in larger parts, but here with more energy and there with less energy, it is in its entirety present both in the whole body and in every part of it. *Letters* 166.2.

6. Control of the body depends upon control of the soul.

359. And it is when the soul serves God that it exercises a right control over the body; and in the soul itself the reason must be subject to God if it is to govern as it ought the passions and other vices. Hence, when a man does not serve God, what justice can we ascribe to him, since in this case his soul cannot exercise a just control over the body, nor his reason over his vices? *City of God* 19.21.

7. The soul is the chief good of the body.

360. Now if we ask what is the chief good of the body, reason obliges us to admit that it is that by means of which the body comes to be in its best state. But of all the things which invigorate the body, there is nothing better or greater than the soul. The chief good of the body, then, is not bodily pleasure, not absence of pain, not strength, not beauty, not swiftness, or whatever else is usually reckoned among the goods of the body, but simply the soul. *On the Morals of the Catholic Church 5.*

8. The soul is intermediate between God and the body.

361. These things being premised and firmly established—that the rational soul is made happy only by God, that the body is enlivened only by the soul, and that the soul is a something intermediate between God and the body—There is nothing more powerful than this creature, which is called the rational mind, nothing more sublime: whatever is above this, is but the Creator. *On the Gospel of John* 27.6.

9. The first death is the separation of soul and body.

362. For if we look at the matter a little more carefully, we shall see that even when a man dies faithfully and laudably for the truth's sake, it is still death he is avoiding. For he submits to some part of death, for the very purpose of avoiding the whole, and the second and eternal death over and above. He submits to the separation of soul and body, lest the soul be separated both from God and from the body, and so the whole first death be completed, and the second death receive him everlastingly. . . . And regarding what happens after death, it is no absurdity to say that death is good to the good, and evil to the evil. For the disembodied spirits of the just are at rest; but those of the wicked suffer punishment till their bodies rise again—those of the just to life everlasting, and of the others to death eternal, which is called the second death. *City of God* 13.8.

10. The soul made the body sinful.

363. But if any one says that the flesh is the cause of all vices and ill conduct, inasmuch as the soul lives wickedly only because it is moved by the flesh, it is certain he has not carefully considered the whole nature of man. For "the corruptible body, indeed, weigheth down the soul." Whence, too, the apostle, speaking of this corruptible body, of which he had shortly before said, "though our outward man perish," says, "We know that if our earthly house of this tabernacle were dissolved, we have a building of God, an house not made with hands, eternal in the heavens. . . ." *City of God* 14.3.

11. The body is a burden or weight to the soul.

364. We are then burdened with this corruptible body; but knowing that the cause of this burdensomeness is not the nature and substance of the body, but its corruption, we do not desire to be deprived of the body, but to be clothed with its immortality. For then, also, there will be a body, but it shall no longer be a burden, being no longer corruptible. At present, then, "the corruptible body presseth down the soul, and the earthly tabernacle weigheth down the mind that museth upon. . . ." *City of God* 13.13.

365. The soul is weighed down not by the body as such, but by the body such as it has become as a consequence of sin and its punishment. *City of God* 13.16.

366. It is true that "the corruptible body is a load upon the soul...." On the one hand, our corruptible body may be a burden on our soul; on the other hand, the cause of this encumbrance is not in the nature and substance of the body, and, therefore, aware as we are of its corruption, we do not desire to be divested of the body but rather to be clothed with its immortality. *City of God* 14.3.

E. Man's nature is good in itself (see also chapter 8, Evil).

367. From this every one sees, who can see, that every nature, as far as it is nature, is good. . . . *Against the Epistle of Manichaeus* 33.

368. I perceived, therefore, and it was made clear to me, that Thou didst make all things good, nor is there any substance at all that was not made by Thee; and because all that Thou hast made are not equal, therefore all things are; because individually they are good, and altogether very good, because our God made all things very good. *Confessions* 7.12.

369. No nature, therefore, as far as it is nature, is evil; but to each nature there is no evil except to be diminished in respect of good. But if by being diminished it should be consumed so that there is no good, no nature would be left; not only such as the Manichaeans introduce, where so great good things are found that their exceeding blindness is wonderful, but such as any one can introduce. *On the Nature of Good* 17.

F. Man's nature has been corrupted by evil (see also 602-611).

370. And indeed evil had never been, had not the mutable nature—mutable, though good, and created by the most high God and immutable Good, who created all things good—brought evil upon itself by sin. And this its sin is itself proof that its nature was originally good. For had it not been very good, though not equal to its Creator, the desertion of God as its light could not have been an evil to it. For as blindness is a vice of the eye, and this very fact indicates that the eye was created to see the light, and as, consequently, vice itself proves that the eye is more excellent than the other members, because it is capable of light (for on no other supposition would it be a vice of the eye to want light), so the nature which once enjoyed God teaches, even by its very vice, that it was created the best of all, since it is now miserable because it does not enjoy God. *City of God* 22.1.

371. This shows that the natures, as far as they are natures, are good; for when you take from them the good instead of the evil, no natures remain. *City of God* 12.1.

372. From this every one sees, who can see, that every nature, as far as it is nature, is good; since in one and the same thing in which I found something to praise, and he found something to blame, if the good things are taken away, no nature will remain; but if the disagreeable things are taken away, the nature will remain unimpaired. Take from waters their thickness and muddiness, and pure clear water remains; take from them the consistence of their parts, and no water will be left. If then, after the evil is removed, the nature remains in a purer state, and does not remain at all when the good is taken away, it must be the good which makes the nature of the thing in which it is, while the evil is not nature, but contrary to nature. *Against the Epistle of Manichaeus* 33.

III. The fall of man (see also 496–510)

A. The whole human race was involved in original sin.

373. And behold, there was I received by the scourge of bodily sickness, and I was descending into hell burdened with all the sins that I had committed, both against Thee, myself, and others, many and grievous, over and above that bond of original sin whereby we all die in Adam. *Confessions* 5.9.

374. Man's nature, indeed, was created at first faultless and without any sin; but that nature of man in which every one is born from

Adam, now wants the Physician because it is not sound. *On Nature and Grace* 3.

1. The chief nature of Adam's sin was pride.

375. Our first parents fell into open disobedience because already they were secretly corrupted; for the evil act had never been done had not an evil will preceded it. And what is the origin of our evil will but pride? For "pride is the beginning of sin." *City of God* 14.13.

2. Original sin involves a number of sins.

376. However, even in that one sin, which "by one man entered into the world, and so passed upon all men," and on account of which infants are baptized, a number of distinct sins may be observed, if it be analyzed as it were into its separate elements. For there is in it pride, because man chose to be under his own dominion, rather than under the dominion of God; and blasphemy, because he did not believe God; and murder, for he brought death upon himself; and spiritual fornication, for the purity of the human soul was corrupted by the seducing blandishments of the serpent; and theft, for man turned to his own use the food he had been forbidden to touch; and avarice, for he had a craving for more than should have been sufficient for him; and whatever other sin can be discovered on careful reflection to be involved in this one admitted sin. *Enchiridion* 45.

B. Men are born in sin.

377. That infant children, even before they have committed any sin of their own, are partakers of sinful flesh, is, in my opinion, proved by their requiring to have it healed in them also, by the application in their baptism of the remedy provided in Him who came in the likeness of sinful flesh. *Letters* 143.6.

378. We were brought low, became mortal, were filled with fears, with errors; this by desert of sin, with which desert and guilt is every man born. *On the Creed* 2.

379. For whichever of them may justly claim our preference, far be it from us to assail this article of faith, about which we have no uncertainty, that every soul, even the soul of an infant, requires to be delivered from the binding guilt of sin, and that there is no deliverance except through Jesus Christ and Him crucified. *Letters* 166.3.7.

C. Original sin brought condemnation on the entire race.

380. Therefore "death reigned from Adam unto Moses," in all who were not assisted by the grace of Christ, that in them the kingdom of death might be destroyed, "even in those who had not sinned after the similitude of Adam's transgression," that is, who had not yet sinned of their individual will, as Adam did, but had drawn from him original sin, "who is the figure of him that was to come," because in him was constituted the form of condemnation to his future progeny, who should spring from him by nature descent; so that from one all men were born to a condemnation, from which there is no deliverance but in the Saviour's grace. *On Forgiveness of Sins, and Baptism* 1.13.

381. The entire mass, therefore, incurs penalty; and if the deserved punishment of condemnation were rendered to all, it would without doubt be righteously rendered. They, therefore, who are delivered therefrom by grace are called, not vessels of their own merits, but "vessels of mercy." But of whose mercy, if not His who sent Christ Jesus into the world to save sinners, whom He foreknew, and foreordained, and called, and justified, and glorified? *On Nature and Grace* 5.

D. The whole human race was corrupted by original sin.

382. We have already stated in the preceding books that God, desiring not only that the human race might be able by their similarity of nature to associate with one another, but also that they might be bound together in harmony and peace by the ties of relationship, was pleased to derive all men from one individual, and created man with such a nature that the members of the race should not have died, had not the two first (of whom the one was created out of nothing, and the other out of him) merited this by their disobedience; for by them so great a sin was committed, that by it the human nature was altered for the worse, and was transmitted also to their posterity, liable to sin and subject to death. *City of God* 14.1.

383. In the first man, therefore, there existed the whole human nature, which was to be transmitted by the woman to posterity, when that conjugal union received the divine sentence of its own condemnation; and what man was made, not when created, but when he sinned and was punished, this he propagated, so far as the origin of sin and death are concerned. *City of God* 13.3.

384. For God, the author of natures, not of vices, created man upright; but man, being of his own will corrupted, and justly condemned, begot corrupted, and condemned children. For we all were in that one man, since we all were that one man, who fell into sin by the woman who was made from him before the sin. For not yet was the particular form created and distributed to us, in which we as individuals were to live, but already the seminal nature was there from which we were to be propagated; and this being vitiated by sin, and bound by the chain of death, and justly condemned, man could not be born of man in any other state. And thus, from the bad use of free will, there originated the whole train of evil, which, with its concatenation of miseries, convoys the human race from its depraved origin, as from a corrupt, root, on to the destruction of the second death, which has no end, those only being excepted who are freed by the grace of God. *City of God* 13.14.

E. *The human race is wholly corrupted by sin.*

385. That the whole human race has been condemned in its first origin, this life itself, if life it is to be called, bears witness by the host of cruel ills with which it is filled. Is not this proved by the profound and dreadful ignorance which produces all the errors that enfold the children of Adam, and from which no man can be delivered without toil, pain, and fear? Is it not proved by his love of so many vain and hurtful things, which produces gnawing cares, disquiet, griefs, fears, wild joys, quarrels, law-suits, wars, treasons, angers, hatreds, deceit, flattery, fraud, theft, robbery, perfidy, pride, ambition, envy, murders, parricides, cruelty, ferocity, wickedness, luxury, insolence, impudence, shamelessness, fornications, adulteries, incests, and the numberless uncleannesses and unnatural acts of both sexes? *City of God* 22.22.

F. *Original sin resulted in death.*

1. Meaning of *death*

386. Since there is no mention of more than one death in the Scriptural passage: "Thou shalt die the death," we should interpret it to mean that particular death which occurs when the life of the soul (which is God) abandons it. . . . However, although we may take it that God intimated only this one death in the words: "In what day soever thou shalt eat of it, thou shalt die the death," by which He meant: "In whatever day you shall leave me through disobedience I shall leave you without grace," nevertheless, the mention of this one death includes all the other deaths which were certainly to follow. *City of God* 13.15.

2. Two kinds of death

387. When, therefore, God said to that first man whom he had placed in Paradise, referring to the forbidden fruit, "In the days that thou eatest thereof thou shalt surely die," that threatening included not only the first part of the first death, by which the soul is deprived of God; nor only the subsequent part of the first death, by which the soul is deprived of the soul; nor only the whole first death itself, by which the soul is punished in separation from God and from the body;—but it includes whatever of death there is, even to that final death, which is called second, and to which none is subsequent. *City of God* 13.12.

388. For the first consists of two; the second is the complete death, which consists of all. For, as the whole earth consists of many lands, and the Church universal of many churches, so death universal consists of all deaths. The first consists of two, one of the body, and another of the soul. So that the first death is a death of the whole man, since the soul without God and without the body suffers punishment for a time; but the second is when the soul, without God but with the body, suffers punishment everlasting. *City of God* 13.12.

G. *The soul lost its mastery over the body.*

389. For, as soon as our first parents had transgressed the commandment, divine grace forsook them, and they were confounded at their own wickedness; and therefore they took figleaves (which were possibly the first that came to hand in their troubled state of mind), and covered their shame; for though their members remained the same, they had shame now where they had none before. They experienced a new motion of their flesh, which had become disobedient to them, in strict retribution of their own disobedience to God. For the soul, revelling in its own liberty, and scorning to serve God, was itself deprived of the command it had formerly maintained over the body. And because it had willfully deserted its superior Lord, it no longer held its own inferior servant; neither could it hold the flesh subject, as it would always have been able to do had it remained itself subject to God. Then began the flesh to lust against the Spirit, in which strife we are born, deriving from the first transgression a seed of death, and bearing in our members, and in our vitiated nature, the contest or even victory of the flesh. *City of God* 13.13.

6

Salvation

I. God and salvation

A. *The order of God's decrees*

1. God's absolute eternal knowledge excludes a sequence in decrees.

390. It is not as if the knowledge of God were of various kinds, knowing in different ways things which as yet are not, things which are, and things which have been. For not in our fashion does He look forward to what is future, nor at what is present, nor back upon what is past; but in a manner quite different and far and profoundly remote from our way of thinking. For He does not pass from this to that by transition of thought, but beholds all things with absolute unchangeableness; so that of those things which emerge in time, the future, indeed, are not yet, and the present are now, and the past no longer are; but all of these are by Him comprehended in His stable and eternal presence. *City of God* 11.21.

2. God's unchangeable will excludes a sequence in decrees.

391. Thus His saints, inspired by His holy will, desire many things which never happen. They pray, e.g. for certain individuals—they pray in a pious and holy manner—but what they request He does not perform, though He Himself by His own Holy Spirit has wrought in them this will to pray. And consequently, when the saints, in conformity with God's mind, will and pray that all men be saved, we can use this mode of expression: God wills and does not perform—

meaning that He who causes them to will these things Himself wills them. But if we speak of that will of His which is eternal as His foreknowledge, certainly He has already done all things in heaven and on earth that He has willed—not only past and present things, but even things still future. But before the arrival of that time in which He has willed the occurrence of what He foreknew and arranged before all time, we say, It will happen when God wills. But if we are ignorant not only of the time in which it is to be, but even whether it shall be at all, we say, It will happen if God wills—not because God will then have a new will which He had not before, but because that event, which from eternity has been prepared in His unchangeable will, shall then come to pass. *City of God* 22.2.

392. For altogether as Thou art, Thou only knowest, Who are unchangeably, and knowest unchangeably, and willest unchangeably. And Thy Essence Knoweth and Willeth unchangeably; and Thy Knowledge Is, and Willeth unchangeably; and Thy Will Is, and Knoweth unchangeably. Nor doth it appear just to Thee, that as the Unchangeable Light knoweth Itself, so should It be known by that which is enlightened and changeable. Therefore unto Thee is my soul as "land where no water is," because as it cannot of itself enlighten itself, so it cannot of itself satisfy itself. For so is the fountain of life with Thee, like as in Thy light we shall see light. *Confessions* 13.16.

3. God's eternal will excludes a sequence in decrees.

393. For if any new motion has arisen in God, and a new will, to form a creature which He had never before formed, however can that be a true eternity where there ariseth a will which was not before? For the will of God is not a creature, but before the creature; because nothing could be created unless the will of the Creator were before it. The will of God, therefore pertaineth to His very Substance. But if anything hath arisen in the Substance of God which was not before, that Substance is not truly called eternal. But if it was the eternal will of God that the creature should be, why was not the creature also from eternity? *Confessions* 11.10.

4. God's simplicity excludes a sequence in decrees.

394. Lo, are they not full of their ancient way, who say to us, "What was God doing before He made heaven and earth? For if," say they,

"He were unoccupied, and did nothing, why does He not for ever also, and from henceforth, cease from working, as in times past He did? For if any new motion has arisen in God, and a new will, to form a creature which He had never before formed, however can that be a true eternity where there ariseth a will which was not before? For the will of God is not a creature, but before the creature; because nothing could be created unless the will of the Creator were before it . . . ?"

Those who say these things do not as yet understand Thee. . . . They even endeavor to comprehend things eternal; but as yet their heart flieth about in the past and future motions of things, and is still wavering. Who shall hold it and fix it, that it may rest a little, and by degrees catch the glory of the ever-standing eternity and compare it with the times which never stand, and see that it is incomparable. . . . *Confessions* 11.10,11.

B. Predestination

1. *Predestination* is defined.

395. This is the predestination of the saints—nothing else; to wit, the foreknowledge and the preparation of God's kindnesses, whereby they are most certainly delivered, whoever they are that are delivered. But where are the rest left by the righteous divine judgment except in the mass of ruin, where the Tyrians and the Sidonians were left? who, moreover, might have believed if they had seen Christ's wonderful miracles. But since it was not given to them to believe, the means of believing also were denied them. *On the Gift of Perseverance* 25.

2. *Predestination* is synonymous with *foreknowledge*.

396. Consequently sometimes the same predestination is signified also under the name of foreknowledge; as says the apostle, "God has not rejected His people whom He foreknew." Here, when he says "He foreknew," the sense is not rightly understood except as "He predestined," as is shown by the context of the passage itself. For he was speaking of the remnant of the Jews which were saved; while the rest perished. *On the Gift of Perseverance* 41.

3. God predestines some to destruction.

397. They are sheep through believing, sheep in following the Shepherd, sheep in not despising their Redeemer, sheep in entering by the door, sheep in going out and finding pasture, sheep in the enjoyment of eternal life. What did He mean, then, in saying to them, "Ye are not of my sheep"? That He saw them predestined to everlasting destruction, not won to eternal life by the price of His own blood. *On the Gospel of John* 48.4.

398. "There is none that doeth good, no, not one," unless that the Psalmist there censures some one nation, amongst whom there was not a man that did good, wishing to remain "children of men," and not sons of God, by whose grace man becomes good, in order to do good? For we must suppose the Psalmist here to mean that "good" which he describes in the context, saying, "God looked down from heaven upon the children of men, to see if there were any that did understand, and seek God." Such good then as this, seeking after God, there was not a man found who pursued it, no, not one; but this was in that class of men which is predestined to destruction. It was upon such that God looked down in His foreknowledge, and passed sentence. *On Man's Perfection in Righteousness* 13.

4. God predestines some to life, some to death.

399. How much better, then, is it, that I should not separately dispute and affirm about the soul, what I am ignorant of; but simply hold what I see the apostle has most plainly taught us. That owing to one man all pass into condemnation who are born of Adam unless they are born again in Christ, even as He has appointed them to be regenerated, before they die in the body, whom He predestined to everlasting life, as the most merciful bestower of grace; whilst to those whom He has predestined to eternal death, He is also the most righteous awarder of punishment, not only on account of the sins which they add in the indulgence of their own will, but also because of their original sin, even if, as in the case of infants, they add nothing thereto. Now this is my definite view on that question, so that the hidden things of God may keep their secret, without impairing my own faith. *On the Soul and Its Origin* 4.16.

5. The number of the predestined is certain.

400. I speak thus of those who are predestined to the kingdom of God, whose number is so certain that one can neither be added to them nor taken from them: not of those who, when He had announced and spoken, were multiplied beyond number. For they may be said to be called but not chosen, because they are not called according to the purpose. But that the number of the elect is certain, and neither to be increased nor diminished. *On Rebuke and Grace* 39.

6. The predestined fill up the ranks of fallen angels.

401. God elected men to fill in gaps left by fallen angels and so it pleased God, the Creator, and Governor of the universe, that, since the whole body of the angels had not fallen into rebellion, the part of them which had fallen should remain in perdition eternally, and that the other part, which had in the rebellion remained steadfastly loyal, should rejoice in the sure and certain knowledge of their eternal happiness; but that, on the other hand, mankind, who constituted the remainder of the intelligent creation, having perished without exception under sin, both original and actual, and the consequent punishments, should be in part restored, and should fill up the gap which the rebellion and fall of the devils had left in the company of the angels. For this is the promise to the saints, that at the resurrection they shall be equal to the angels of God. *Enchiridion* 29.

C. Election

1. Election is according to God's purpose.

402. Of these no one perishes, because all are elected. And they are elected because they were called according to the purpose—the purpose, however, not their own, but God's; of which He elsewhere says, "That the purpose of God according to election might stand, not of works but of Him that calleth, it was said unto her that the elder shall serve the younger." *On Rebuke and Grace* 14.

403. Therefore God chose us in Christ before the foundation of the world, predestinating us to the adoption of children, not because we were going to be of ourselves holy and immaculate, but He chose and predestinated us that we might be so. Moreover, He did this according to the good pleasure of His will, so that nobody might glory concerning his own will, but about God's will towards himself. He did this according to the riches of His grace, according to His good will, which He purposed in His beloved Son, in whom we have obtained a share, being predestinated according to the purpose, not ours, but His, who worketh all things to such an extent as that He worketh in us to will also. Moreover, He worketh according to the counsel of His will, that we may be to the praise of His glory. For this reason it is that we cry that no one should glory in man, and, thus, not in himself; but whoever glorieth let him glory in the Lord, that he may be for the praise of His glory. Because He Himself worketh according to His purpose that we may be to the praise of His glory, and, of course, holy and immaculate, for which purpose He called us, predestinating us before the foundation of the world. Out of this, His purpose, is that special calling of the elect for whom He co-worketh with all things for good, because they are called according to His purpose, and "the gifts and calling of God are without repentance." *On the Predestination of the Saints* 37.

> 2. God's elective purpose is to restore all things to Christ for God's glory.

404. In this mystery of His will, He placed the riches of His grace, according to His good pleasure, not according to ours, which could not possibly be good unless He Himself, according to His own good pleasure, should aid it to become so. But when [the apostle] had said, "According to His good pleasure," he added, "which He purposed in Him," that is, in His beloved Son, "in the dispensation of the fulness of times to restore all things in Christ, which are in heaven, and which are in earth, in Him: in whom also we too have obtained a lot, being predestinated according to the counsel of His will; that we should be to the praise of His glory." *On the Predestination of the Saints* 36.

> 3. God's purpose coincides with the wills of angels and men (see chapter 7, Free Will).

405. But however strong may be the purposes either of angels or of men, whether of good or bad, whether these purposes fall in with the will of God or run counter to it, the will of the Omnipotent is never defeated; and His will never can be evil; because even when it inflicts evil it is just, and what is just is certainly not evil. The omnipotent God, then, whether in mercy He pitieth whom He will, or in judgment hardeneth whom He will, is never unjust in what He does, never does anything except of His own free-will, and never wills anything that He does not perform. *Enchiridion* 102.

4. God's purpose is to bring good out of evil.

406. For whatever the wicked freely do through blind and unbridled lust, and whatever they suffer against their will in the way of open punishment, this all evidently pertains to the just wrath of God. But the goodness of the Creator never fails either to supply life and vital power to the wicked angels (without which their existence would soon come to an end); or, in the case of mankind, who spring from a condemned and corrupt stock, to impart form and life to their seed, to fashion their members, and through the various seasons of their life, and in the different parts of the earth, to quicken their senses, and bestow upon them the nourishment they need. For He judged it better to bring good out of evil, than not to permit any evil to exist. *Enchiridion* 27.

407. Since then, God was not ignorant that man would fall, why should He not have suffered him to be tempted by an angel who hated and envied him? It was not indeed, that He was unaware that he should be conquered, but because He foresaw that to the man's seed, aided by divine grace, this same devil himself should be conquered, to the greater glory of the saints. All was brought about in such a manner, that neither did any future event escape God's foreknowledge nor did His foreknowledge compel any one to sin, and so as to demonstrate in the experience of the intelligent creation, human and angelic, how great a difference there is between the private presumption of the creature and the Creator's protection. For who will dare to believe or say that it was not God's power to prevent both angels and men from sinning? But God preferred to leave this in their power, and thus to show both what evil could be wrought by their pride, and what good by His grace. *City of God* 14.27.

5. God's election is sure as He is sure.

408. He wishes these, therefore, to be understood whom He called according to His purpose, lest any among them should be thought to be called and not elected, on account of that sentence of the Lord's: "Many are called but few are elected." For whoever are elected are without doubt also called; but not whosoever are called are as a consequence elected. Those, then, are elected, as has often been said, who are called according to the purpose who also are pre-destinated and foreknown. If any one of these perishes, God is mistaken; but none of them perishes, because God is not mistaken. If any one of these perish, God is overcome by human sin; but none of them perishes, because God is overcome by nothing. *On Rebuke and Grace* 14.

II. Christ and salvation

A. *Christ: the basis of true universal faith*

409. Here surely is an answer to your question as to what is the starting-point, and what the goal: we begin in faith, and are made perfect by sight. This also is the sum of the whole body of doctrine. But the sure and proper foundation of the catholic faith is Christ. *Enchiridion* 5.

B. *The extent of Christ's atonement*

1. Christ's atonement extends to all who believe.

410. For as the clause, "By the offence of one, upon all men to condemnation," is so worded that not one is omitted in its sense, so in the corresponding clause, "By righteousness of One, upon all men unto justification of life," no one is omitted in its sense,—not, indeed, because all men have faith and are washed in His baptism, but because no man is justified unless he believes in Christ and is cleansed by His baptism. The term "all" is therefore used in a way which shows that no one whatever can be supposed able to be saved by any other means than through Christ Himself. For if in a city there be appointed but one instructor, we are most correct in saying: That man teaches all in that place; not meaning, indeed, that all who live in the city take lessons of him, but that no one is instructed unless taught by him. In like manner no one is justified unless Christ has justified him. *On Nature and Grace* 48.

2. Christ's death is effectual throughout the whole world.

411. For he that has said, "We have Jesus Christ the righteous, and He is the propitiation for our sins," having an eye to those who would divide themselves, and would say, "Lo, here is Christ, lo, there," and would show Him in a part who bought the whole and possesses the whole, he forthwith goes on to say, "Not our sins only, but also the sins of the whole world." What is this, brethren? Certainly "we have found it in the fields of the woods," we have found the Church in all nations. Behold, Christ "is the propitiation for our sins; not ours only, but also the sins of the whole world." Behold, thou hast the Church throughout the whole world; do not follow false justifiers who in truth are cutters off. Be thou in that mountain which hath filled the whole earth: because "Christ is the propitiation for our sins; not only ours, but also the sins of the whole world," which He hath bought with His blood. *On the Gospel of John* 1.8.

412. But what shall I say, brethren? Let us see plainly what He purchased. For there He bought, where He paid the price. Paid it for how much? If He paid it only for Africa, let us be Donatists, and not be called Donatists, but Christians; since Christ bought only Africa: although even here are other than Donatists. But He has not been silent of what He bought in this transaction. . . . Hear ye what He bought: "All the ends of the earth shall remember, and turn unto the Lord; and all the kindreds of the nations shall worship in His sight: for the kingdom is His, and He shall rule the nations." Behold what it is He has bought! Behold! "For God, the King of all the earth," is thy Bridegroom. Why, then, wouldst thou have one so rich reduced to rags? Acknowledge Him: He bought the whole; yet thou sayest, "Thou hast a part of it here." *On the Gospel of John* 13.14.

3. Christ's atonement is not effectual for those
who would deny His humanity.

413. Whoever, therefore, acknowledges Christ as God, and disowns Him as man, Christ died not for him; for as man it was that Christ died. He who disowns Christ as man, finds no reconciliation to God by the Mediator. For there is one God, and one Mediator between God and men, the man Christ Jesus. He that denies Christ as man is not justified: for as by the disobedience of one man, many were made sinners; so also by the obedience of one man shall many be made righteous. He that denies Christ as man, shall not rise again into the resurrection of life; for by man is death, and by man is also the resurrection of the dead: for as in Adam all die, even so in Christ shall all be made alive. And by what means is He the Head of the Church, but by His manhood, because the Word was made flesh? that is, God, the Only-begotten of God the Father, became man. And how then can one be in the body of Christ who denies the man Christ? Or how can one be a member who disowns the Head? *On the Gospel of John* 66.2.

4. Christ's death extends to elect infants (see 399, 469).

414. Now, if infants are not embraced within this reconciliation and salvation, who wants them for the baptism of Christ? But if they are embraced, then are they reckoned as among the dead for whom He died; nor can they be possibly reconciled and saved by Him, unless He remit and impute not unto them their sins. *On Forgiveness of Sins, and Baptism* 1.44.

5. Christ took away the original sin and all others added to it.

415. With this difference: the first man brought one sin into the world, but this man took away not only that one sin, but all that He found added to it. *Enchiridion* 50.

C. The nature of Christ's atonement: penal substitution

1. Christ satisfied God's wrath.

416. And so the human race was lying under a just condemnation and all men were the children of wrath. Of which wrath it is written: "All our days are passed away in Thy wrath; we spend our years as a tale that is told." Of which wrath also Job says: "Man that is born of a woman is of few days, and full of trouble." Of which wrath also the Lord Jesus says: "He that believeth on the Son hath everlasting life:

and he that believeth not the Son shall not see life; but the wrath of
God abideth on him." He does not say it will come, but it "abideth on
him." For every man is born with it; wherefore the apostle says: "We
were by nature the children of wrath, even as others." Now, as men
were lying under this wrath by reason of their original sin, and as
this original sin was the more heavy and deadly in proportion to the
number and magnitude of the actual sins which were added to it,
there was need for a Mediator, that is, for a reconciler, who, by the
offering of one sacrifice, of which all the sacrifices of the law and the
prophets were types, should take away this wrath. Wherefore the
apostle says: "For if, when we were enemies, we were reconciled to
God by the death of His Son, much more, being reconciled, we shall
be saved by His life." Now when God is said to be angry, we do not
attribute to Him such a disturbed feeling as exists in the mind of an
angry man; but we call His just displeasure against sin by the name
"anger," a word transferred by analogy from human emotions. But
our being reconciled to God through a Mediator, and receiving the
Holy Spirit, so that we who were enemies are made sons ("For as
many as are led by the Spirit of God, they are the sons of God"): this
is the grace of God through Jesus Christ our Lord. *Enchiridion* 33.

2. Christ's death stands in relation to the Father.

a) Christ died because of the Father's command.

417. And, as if it were said to Him, Why, then, dost Thou die, if Thou
hast no sin to merit the punishment of death? He immediately
added, "But that the world may know that I love the Father, and as
the Father gave me commandment, even so I do: arise, let us go
hence." For He was sitting at table with those who were similarly
occupied. But "let us go," He said, and whither, but to the place
where He, who had nothing in Him deserving of death, was to be
delivered up to death? But He had the Father's commandment to
die, as the very One of whom it had been foretold, "Then I paid for
that which I took not away;" and so appointed to pay death to the
full, while owing it nothing, and to redeem us from the death that
was our due. *On the Gospel of John* 79.2.

b) Christ died in obedience to the Father.

418. As to his statement, indeed, that "the Lord was able to die
without sin;" His being born also was of the ability of His mercy, not

the demand of His nature: so, likewise, did He undergo death of His own power; and this is our price which He paid to redeem us from death. Now, this truth their contention labours hard to make of none effect; for human nature is maintained by them to be such, that with free will it wants no such ransom in order to be translated from the power of darkness and of him who has the power of death, into the kingdom of Christ the Lord. And yet, when the Lord drew near His passion, He said, "Behold, the prince of this world cometh, and shall find nothing in me,"—and therefore no sin, of course, on account of which he might exercise dominion over Him, so as to destroy Him. "But," added He, "that the world may know that I do the will of my Father, arise, let us go hence;" as much as to say, I am going to die, not through the necessity of sin, but in voluntariness of obedience. *On Nature and Grace* 26.

> c) *Christ's death was a joint venture*
> *between the Father and the Son.*

419. But what is meant by "justified in His blood"? What power is there in this blood, I beseech you, that they who believe should be justified in it? And what is meant by "being reconciled by the death of His Son?" Was it indeed so, that when God the Father was wroth with us, He saw the death of His Son for us, and was appeased towards us? Was then His Son already so far appeased towards us, that He even deigned to die for us; while the Father was still so far wroth, that except His Son died for us, He would not be appeased? And what, then, is that which the same teacher of the Gentiles himself says in another place: "What shall we then say to these things? If God be for us, who can be against us? He that spared not His own Son, but delivered Him up for us all; how has He not with Him also freely given us all things?" Pray, unless the Father had been already appeased, would He have delivered up His own Son, not sparing Him for us? Does not this opinion seem to be as it were contrary to that? In the one, the Son dies for us, and the Father is reconciled to us by His death; in the other, as though the Father first loved us, He Himself on our account does not spare the Son, He Himself for us delivers Him up to death. But I see that the Father loved us also before, not only before the Son died for us, but before He created the world; the apostle himself being witness, who says, "According as He hath chosen us in Him before the foundation of the world." Nor was the Son delivered up for us as it were unwillingly, the Father Himself not sparing Him, "Who loved me, and delivered up Himself for me." Therefore together both the Father and the Son, and the Spirit of both, work all things equally and harmoniously; yet we are justified in the blood of Christ, and we are reconciled to God by the death of His Son. *On the Trinity* 13.11.

3. Christ is the sin offering.

a) Christ was called "sin" as the sin offering.

420. But perhaps, through some special perception of my own, I have said that sin is a sacrifice for sin. Let those who have read it be free to acknowledge it; let not those who have not read it be backward; let them not, I say, be backward to read that they may be truthful in judging. For when God gave commandment about the offering of sacrifices for sin, in which sacrifices there was no expiation of sins, but the shadow of things to come, the self-same sacrifices, the self-same offerings, the self-same victims, the self-same animals, which were brought forward to be slain for sins, and in whose blood that [true] blood was prefigured, are themselves called sins by the law; and that to such an extent that in certain passages it is written in these terms, that the priests, when about to sacrifice, were to lay their hands on the head of the sin, that is, on the head of the victim about to be sacrificed for sin. Such sin, then, that is, such a sacrifice for sin, was our Lord Jesus Christ made, "who knew no sin." *On the Gospel of John* 41.6.

b) Christ was the substitutionary sin offering.

421. So sin means both a bad action deserving punishment, and death the consequence of sin. Christ has no sin in the sense of deserving death, but He bore for our sakes sin in the sense of death as brought on human nature by sin. . . . By Christ's taking our sin in this sense, its condemnation is our deliverance, while to remain in subjection to sin is to be condemned. *Reply to Faustus the Manichaean* 14.3.

c) Offering was rendered to God, not to creature,
thus disallowing the ransom-to-Satan theory.

422. And hence that true Mediator, in so far as, by assuming the form of a servant, He became the Mediator between God and men, the man Christ Jesus, though in the form of God He received sacrifice together with the Father, with whom He is one God, yet in the form of a servant. He chose rather to be than to receive a sacrifice, that not even by this instance any one might have occasion to suppose that sacrifice should be rendered to any creature. Thus He is both the Priest who offers and the Sacrifice offered. *City of God* 10.20.

D. The effects of Christ's atonement

1. Christ delivered man from the power of the devil.

423. The devil, therefore, had possession of the human race, and held them by the written bond of their sins as criminals amenable to punishment; he ruled in the hearts of unbelievers, and, deceiving and enslaving them, seduced them to forsake the Creator and give worship to the creature; but by faith in Christ, which was confirmed by His death and resurrection, and, by His blood, which was shed for the remission of sins, thousands of believers are delivered from the dominion of the devil, are united to the body of Christ, and under this great head are made His faithful members. This it was that He called the judgment, this righteous separation, this expulsion of the devil from His own redeemed. *On the Gospel of John* 52.6.

424. For baptism found in Him nothing to wash away, as death found in Him nothing to punish; so that it was in the strictest justice, and not by the mere violence of power, that the devil was crushed and conquered: for, as he had most unjustly put Christ to death, though there was no sin in Him to deserve death, it was most just that through Christ he should lose his hold of those who by sin were justly subject to the bondage in which he held them. Both of these, then, that is, both baptism and death, were submitted to by Him, not through a pitiable necessity, but of His own free pity for us, and as part of an arrangement by which, as one man brought sin into the world, that is, upon the whole human race, so one man was to take away the sin of the world. *Enchiridion* 49.

2. Christ brought peace between heaven and earth.

425. Yet what was done for the redemption of man through His death was in a sense done for the angels, because the enmity which sin had put between men and the holy angels is removed, and friendship is restored between them, and by the redemption of man the gaps which the great apostasy left in the angelic host are filled up. *Enchiridion* 61.

426. The things which are in heaven are gathered together when what was lost therefrom in the fall of the angels is restored from among men; and the things which are on earth are gathered together, when those who are predestined to eternal life are redeemed from their old corruption. And thus, through that single sacrifice in which the Mediator was offered up, the one sacrifice of which the many victims under the law were types, heavenly things are brought into peace with earthly things, and earthly things with heavenly. *Enchiridion* 62.

3. Christ brought the benefits of resurrection and glorification for men.

a) *He effects the resurrection of saints.*

427. Accordingly all shall rise in the stature they either had attained or would have attained had they lived to their prime, although it will be no great disadvantage even if the form of the body be infantine or aged, while no infirmity shall remain in the mind nor in the body itself. So that even if any one contends that every person will rise again in the same bodily form in which he died, we need not spend much labor in disputing with him. *City of God* 17.16.

428. But the body, being as it were the outward man, the longer this life lasts is so much the more corrupted, either by age or by disease, or by various afflictions, until it come to that last affliction which all call death. And its resurrection is delayed until the end; when also our justification itself shall be perfected ineffably. For then we shall be like Him, for we shall see Him as He is. *On the Trinity* 4.3.

b) *Ultimate glorification will result when He returns.*

429. But what we believe as to Christ's action in the future, when He shall come from heaven to judge the quick and the dead, has no bearing upon the life which we now lead here; for it forms no part of what He shall do at the end of the world. And it is to this that the apostle refers in what immediately follows the passage quoted above:

"When Christ, who is our life, shall appear, then shall ye also appear with Him in glory." *Enchiridion* 54.

> c) *After the resurrection of believers there will be no power or desire to sin.*

430. After the resurrection, however, when the final, universal judgment has been completed, there shall be two kingdoms, each with its own distinct boundaries, the one Christ's, the other the devil's; the one consisting of the good, the other of the bad,—both, however, consisting of angels and men. The former shall have no will, the latter no power, to sin, and neither shall have any power to choose death; but the former shall live truly and happily in eternal life, the latter shall drag a miserable existence in eternal death without the power of dying; for the life and the death shall both be without end. But among the former there shall be degrees of happiness, one being more pre-eminently happy than another; and among the latter there shall be degrees of misery, one being more endurably miserable than another. *Enchiridion* 111.

431. But in the future life it shall not be in his power to will evil; and yet this will constitute no restriction on the freedom of his will. On the contrary, his will shall be much freer when it shall be wholly impossible for him to be the slave of sin. We should never think of blaming the will, or saying that it was not to be called free, when we so desire happiness, that not only do we shrink from misery, but find it utterly impossible to do otherwise. As, then, the soul even now finds it impossible to desire unhappiness, so in future it shall be wholly impossible for it to desire sin. But God's arrangement was not to be broken, according to which He willed to show how good is a rational being who is able even to refrain from sin, and yet how much better is one who cannot sin at all; just as that was an inferior sort of immortality, and yet it was immortality, when it was possible for man to avoid death, although there is reserved for the future a more perfect immortality, when it shall be impossible for man to die. *Enchiridion* 105.

> d) *Christ was sacrificed to wash away sin.*

432. Begotten and conceived, then, without any indulgence of carnal lust, and therefore bringing with Him no original sin, and by the grace of God joined and united in a wonderful and unspeakable way in one person with the Word, the Only-begotten of the Father, a son by nature, not by grace, and therefore having no sin of His own; nevertheless, on account of the likeness of sinful flesh in which He came, He was called sin, that He might be sacrificed to wash away sin. *Enchiridion* 41.

433. For when on the day of Pentecost the Holy Spirit fell upon an assembly of one hundred and twenty men, among whom were all the apostles; and when they, filled therewith, were speaking in the language of every nation; a goodly number of those who had hated, amazed at the magnitude of the miracle (especially when they perceived in Peter's address so great and divine a testimony borne in behalf of Christ, as that He, who was slain by them and accounted amongst the dead, was proved to have risen again, and to be now alive), were pricked in their hearts and converted; and so became aware of the beneficent character of that precious blood which had been so impiously and cruelly shed, because themselves redeemed by the very blood which they had shed. For the blood of Christ was shed so efficaciously for the remission of all sins, that it could wipe out even the very sin of shedding it. *On the Gospel of John* 92.1.

e) Christ's death brought reconciliation of man to God.

434. He does not say, as some incorrect copies read, "He who knew no sin did sin for us," as if Christ had Himself sinned for our sakes; but he says, "Him who knew no sin," that is, Christ, God, to whom we are to be reconciled, "hath made to be sin for us," that is, hath made Him a sacrifice for our sins by which we might be reconciled to God, He, then, being made sin, just as we are made righteousness (our righteousness being not our own, but God's, not in ourselves, but in Him); He being made sin, not His own, but ours, not in Himself, but in us, showed, by the likeness of sinful flesh in which He was crucified, that though sin was not in Him, yet that in a certain sense He died to sin, by dying in the flesh which was the likeness of sin; and that although He Himself had never lived the old life of sin, yet by His resurrection He typified our new life springing up out of the old death in sin. *Enchiridion* 41.

f) Christ's death leads to everlasting life.

435. What is this? A death is gazed on, that death may have no power. But whose death? The death of life: if it may be said, the death of life; ay, for it may be said, but said wonderfully. But should it not be spoken, seeing it was a thing to be done? Shall I hesitate to utter that which the Lord has deigned to do for me? Is not Christ the life? And yet Christ hung on the cross. Is not Christ life? And yet Christ was dead. But in Christ's death, death died. Life dead slew death; the fullness of life swallowed up death; death was absorbed in the body of Christ. So also shall we say in the resurrection, when now triumphant we shall sing, "Where, O death, is thy contest? Where, O death, is thy sting?" Meanwhile, brethren, that we may be healed from sin, let us now gaze on Christ crucified; for "as Moses," saith He, "lifted up the serpent in the wilderness, so must the Son of man be lifted up; that whosoever believeth on Him may not perish, but have everlasting life." *On the Gospel of John* 12.11.

E. Christ as priest-mediator

1. The mediator was prophesied to rise again.

436. About His resurrection also the oracles of the Psalms are by no means silent. For what else is it that is sung in His person in the 3d Psalm, "I laid me down and took a sleep, [and] I awaked, for the Lord shall sustain me?" Is there perchance any one so stupid as to believe that the prophet chose to point it out to us as something great that He had slept and risen up, unless that sleep had been death, and that awaking the resurrection, which behoved to be thus prophesied concerning Christ? For in the 41st Psalm also it is shown much more clearly, where in the person of the Mediator, in the usual way, things are narrated as if past which were prophesied as yet to come, since these things which were yet to come were in the predestination and foreknowledge of God as if they were done, because they were certain. *City of God* 17.18.

2. An incarnate mediator was necessary.

437. For we could not be redeemed, even through the one Mediator between God and men, the man Christ Jesus, if He were not also God. Now when Adam was created, he, being a righteous man, had no need of a mediator. But when sin had placed a wide gulf between God and the human race, it was expedient that a Mediator, who alone of the human race was born, lived, and died without sin, should reconcile us to God. *Enchiridion* 108.

> 3. Christ was the true mediator (joined to God
> in justice and to man in death).

438. But the true Mediator, whom in Thy secret mercy Thou hast pointed out to the humble, and didst send, that by His example also they might learn the same humility—that "Mediator between God and men, the man Christ Jesus," appeared between mortal sinners and the immortal Just One—mortal with men, just with God; that because the reward of righteousness is life and peace, He might, by righteousness conjoined with God, cancel the death of justified sinners, which He willed to have in common with them. Hence He was pointed out to holy men of old; to the intent that they, through faith in His Passion to come, even as we through faith in that which is past, might be saved. For as man He was Mediator; but as the Word He was not between, because equal to God, and God with God, and together with the Holy Spirit one God. *Confessions* 10.43.

> 4. Christ was both priest and sacrifice.

439. How hast Thou loved us, for whom He, who thought it no robbery to be equal with Thee, "became obedient unto death, even the death of the cross;" He alone "free among the dead," that had power to lay down His life, and power to take it again; for us was He unto Thee both Victor and Victim, and the Victor as being the Victim; for us was He unto Thee both Priest and Sacrifice, and Priest as being the Sacrifice; of slaves making us Thy sons, by being born of Thee, and serving us. *Confessions* 10.43.

440. And what could be so acceptably offered and taken, as the flesh of our sacrifice, made the body of our priest? In such wise that, whereas four things are to be considered in every sacrifice,—to whom it is offered, by whom it is offered, what is offered, for whom it is offered,—the same One and true Mediator Himself, reconciling us to God by the sacrifice of peace, might remain one with Him to whom He offered, might make those one in Himself for whom He offered, Himself might be in one both the offerer and the offering. *On the Trinity* 4.14.

5. Christ as mediator blots out sin.

441. Nevertheless, that one sin, admitted into a place where such perfect happiness reigned, was of so heinous a character, that in one man the whole human race was originally, and as one may say, radically, condemned; and it cannot be pardoned and blotted out except through the one Mediator between God and men, the man Christ Jesus, who only has had power to be so born as not to need a second birth. *Enchiridion* 48.

F. The necessity of Christ's incarnation for His death

1. Augustine previously doubted the incarnation.

442. And our very Saviour Himself, also, Thine only-begotten, I believed to have been reached forth, as it were, for our salvation out of the lump of Thy most effulgent mass, so as to believe nothing of Him but what I was able to imagine in my vanity. Such a nature, then, I thought could not be born of the Virgin Mary without being mingled with the flesh; and how that which I had thus figured to myself could be mingled without being contaminated, I saw not. I was afraid, therefore, to believe Him to be born in the flesh, lest I should be compelled to believe Him contaminated by the flesh. Now will Thy spiritual one blandly and lovingly smile at me if they shall read these my confessions; yet such was I. *Confessions* 5.10.

2. The incarnation of Christ is verified by Scripture.

443. The reason of our believing Him to have been born of the Virgin Mary, is not that He could not otherwise have appeared among men in a true body, but because it is so written in the Scripture, which we must believe in order to be Christians, or to be saved. We believe, then, that Christ was born of the Virgin Mary, because it is so written in the Gospel; we believe that He died on the cross, because it is so written in the Gospel; we believe that both His birth and death were real, because the Gospel is no fiction. *Reply to Faustus the Manichaean* 26.7.

3. Christ is the incarnate principle by which men
are cleansed.

444. It was therefore truly said that man is cleansed only by a Principle, although the Platonists erred in speaking in the plural of principles. But Porphyry, being under the dominion of these envious powers, whose influence he was at once ashamed of and afraid to throw off, refused to recognize that Christ is the Principle by whose incarnation we are purified. Indeed he despised Him, because of the flesh itself which He assumed, that He might offer a sacrifice for our purification,—a great mystery, unintelligible to Porphyry's pride, which that true and benignant Redeemer brought low by His humility, manifesting Himself to mortals by the mortality which He assumed, and which the malignant and deceitful mediators are proud of wanting, promising, as the boon of immortals, a deceptive assistance to wretched men. Thus the good and true Mediator showed that it is sin which is evil, and not the substance or nature of flesh; for this, together with the human soul, could without sin be both assumed and retained, and laid down in death, and changed to something better by resurrection. *City of God* 10.24.

4. Christ is supreme humanity.

445. Since, then, they were written truthfully, I acknowledged a perfect man to be in Christ—not the body of a man only, nor with the body a sensitive soul without a rational, but a very man; whom, not only as being a form of truth, but for a certain great excellency of human nature and a more perfect participation of wisdom, I decided was to be preferred before others. *Confessions* 7.19.

III. The Holy Spirit and salvation

A. God's Holy Spirit is the effectual agent in the effectual call.

1. The Holy Spirit is the source of love and faith in God.

446. Whence, therefore, arises this love,—that is to say, this charity,—by which faith obtained it? For it would not be within us, to what extent soever it is in us, if it were not diffused in our hearts by the Holy Ghost who is given to us. Now "the love of God" is said to be shed abroad in our hearts, not because He loves us, but because He makes us lovers of Himself; just as "the righteousness of God" is used in the sense of our being made righteous by His gift; and "the salvation of the Lord," in that we are saved by Him; and "the faith of Jesus Christ," because He makes us believers in Him. This is that righteousness of God, which He not only teaches us by the precept of His law, but also bestows upon us by the gift of His Spirit. *On the Spirit and the Letter* 56.

2. The Holy Spirit, not fear, leads to salvation by faith.

447. By faith, therefore, in Jesus Christ we obtain salvation—both in so far as it is begun within us in reality, and in so far as its perfection is waited for in hope; "for whosoever shall call on the Lord shall be saved." "How abundant," says the Psalmist, "is the multitude of Thy goodness, O Lord, which Thou hast laid up for them that fear Thee, and hast perfected for them that hope in Thee!" By the law we fear God; by faith we hope in God: but from those who fear punishment grace is hidden. And the soul which labours under this fear, since it has not conquered its evil concupiscence, and from which this fear, like a harsh master, has not departed,—let it flee by faith for refuge to the mercy of God, that He may give it what He commands, and may, by inspiring into it the sweetness of His grace through His Holy Spirit, cause the soul to delight more in what He teaches it, than it delights in what opposes His instruction. *On the Spirit and the Letter* 51.

3. The Holy Spirit produces faith.

448. Speaking of the Holy Ghost, He says, "He shall reprove the world of sin, and of righteousness, and of judgment: of sin, because they have not believed on me: of righteousness, because I go to the Father, and ye shall see me no more." What is that righteousness, whereby men were not to see Him, except that "the just is to live by faith," and that we, not looking at the things which are seen, but at those which are not seen, are to wait in the Spirit for the hope of the righteousness that is by faith? *On Forgiveness of Sins, and Baptism* 2.52.

4. The Holy Spirit justifies us.

449. We have also examined what Thou willedst to be shadowed forth, whether by the creation, or the description of things in such an order. And we have seen that things severally are good, and all things very good, in Thy Word, in Thine Only-Begotten; both heaven and earth, the Head and the body of the Church, in Thy predestination before all times, without morning and evening. But when Thou didst begin to execute in time the things predestinated, that Thou mightest make manifest things hidden, and adjust our disorders (for our sins were over us, and we had sunk into profound darkness away from Thee, and Thy good Spirit was borne over us to help us in due season), Thou didst both justify the ungodly, and didst divide them from the wicked. *Confessions* 13.49.

5. The Holy Spirit regenerates the believer.

450. For His baptism is not with water only, as was that of John, but with the Holy Ghost also; so that whoever believes in Christ is regenerated by that Spirit, of whom Christ being generated, He did not need regeneration. *Enchiridion* 49.

6. The Holy Spirit seals the believer.

451. For when we come to Him, we come to the Father also, because through an equal an equal is known; and the Holy Spirit binds, and as it were seals us, so that we are able to rest permanently in the supreme and unchangeable Good. *On Christian Doctrine* 1.34.

B. God's Holy Spirit is the continuous witness of God's love for man.

1. The gift of the Holy Spirit was confirmed to early believers.

452. For we read nowhere that men spoke in tongues which they did not know, through the Holy Spirit coming upon them; as happened then, when it was needful that His coming should be made plain by visible signs, in order to show that the whole world, and all nations constituted with different tongues, should believe in Christ through the gift of the Holy Spirit. *On the Trinity* 4.29.

2. The Holy Spirit lifts us from the gates of death.

453. In Thy gift we rest; there we enjoy Thee. Our rest is our place. Love lifts us up thither and Thy good Spirit lifteth our lowliness from the gates of death. In Thy good pleasure lies our peace. The body by its own weight gravitates towards its own place. Weight goes not downward only, but to its own place. Fire tends upwards, a stone downwards. They are propelled by their own weights, they seek their own places. Oil poured under the water is raised above the water; water poured upon oil sinks under the oil. They are propelled by their own weights, they seek their own places. Out of order, they are restless; restored to order, they are at rest. My weight is my love; by it am I borne whithersoever I am borne. By Thy Gift we are inflamed, and are borne upwards; we wax hot inwardly, and go forwards. We ascend Thy ways that be in our heart, and sing a song of degrees; we glow inwardly with Thy fire, with Thy good fire, and we go, because we go upwards to the peace of Jerusalem; for glad was I when they said unto me, "Let us go into the house of the Lord." There hath Thy good pleasure placed us, that we may desire no other thing than to dwell there for ever. *Confessions* 13.9.

3. The Holy Spirit shows God's love to man.

454. What then is God's law written by God Himself in the hearts of men, but the very presence of the Holy Spirit, who is "the finger of God," and by whose presence is shed abroad in our hearts the love which is the fulfilling of the law, and the end of the commandment? *On the Spirit and the Letter* 36.

IV. God's revelation and salvation

A. Creation is a witness to the creator.

455. I had heard from the mouth of truth that "there be eunuchs, which have made themselves eunuchs for the kingdom of heaven's sake;" but, saith He, "he that is able to receive it, let him receive it." Vain, assuredly, are all men in whom the knowledge of God is not, and who could not, out of the good things which are seen, find out Him who is good. But I was no longer in that vanity; I had surmounted it, and by the united testimony of Thy whole creation had found Thee, our Creator, and Thy Word, God with Thee and together with Thee and the Holy Ghost one God, by whom Thou createdst all things. *Confessions* 8.1.

B. Scripture is a witness to the Saviour.

1. Scripture is the voice of God (see chapter 2, The Bible).

456. And I sought a way of acquiring strength sufficient to enjoy Thee; but found it not until I embraced that "Mediator between God and man, the man Christ Jesus," "who is over all, God blessed for ever," calling unto me, and saying, "I am the way, the truth, and the life," and mingling that food which I was unable to receive with our flesh. For "the Word was made flesh," that Thy wisdom, by which Thou createdst all things, might provide milk for our infancy. For I did not grasp my Lord Jesus,—I, though humbled, grasped not the humble One; nor did I know what lesson that infirmity of His would teach us. For Thy Word, the Eternal Truth, pre-eminent above the higher parts of Thy creation, raises up those that are subject unto Itself; but in this lower world built for Itself a humble habitation of our clay, whereby He intended to abase from themselves such as would be subjected and bring them over unto Himself, allaying their swelling, and fostering their love; to the end that they might go on no further in self-confidence, but rather should become weak, seeing before their feet the Divinity weak by taking our "coats of skins;" and wearied, might cast themselves down upon It, and It rising, might lift them up. *Confessions* 7.18.

2. The law may be used by the righteous but doesn't make one righteous.

457. For who but a righteous man lawfully uses the law? Yet it is not for him that it is made, but for the unrighteous. Must then the unrighteous man, in order that he may be justified,—that is, become a righteous man,—lawfully use the law, to lead him, as by the schoolmaster's hand, to that grace by which alone he can fulfil what the law commands? Now it is freely that he is justified thereby,—that is, on account of no antecedent merits of his own works; "otherwise grace is no more grace," since it is bestowed on us, not because we have done good works, but that we may be able to do them,—in other words, not because we have fulfilled the law, but in order that we may be able to fulfil the law. . . . Does not the case perhaps stand thus,—nay, not *perhaps*, but rather *certainly*,—that the man who is become righteous thus lawfully uses the law, when he applies it to alarm the unrighteous, so that whenever the disease of some unusual desire begins in them, too, to be augmented by the incentive of the law's prohibition and an increased amount of transgression, they may in faith flee for refuge to the grace that justifies, and becoming delighted with the sweet pleasures of holiness, may escape the penalty of the law's menacing letter through the spirit's soothing gift? In this way the two statements will not be contrary, nor will they be repugnant to each other: even the righteous man may lawfully use a good law, and yet the law be not made for the righteous man; for it is not by the law that he becomes righteous, but by the law of faith, which led him to believe that no other resource was possible to his weakness for fulfilling the precepts which "the law of works" commanded, except to be assisted by the grace of God. *On the Spirit and the Letter* 16.

3. The law points out transgressions and aids
in pointing men to God's grace.

458. The Scriptures of the New Testament, wherein we learn that the intention of the law in its censure is this, that, by reason of the transgressions which men commit, they may flee for refuge to the grace of the Lord, who has pity upon them—"the schoolmaster" "shutting them up unto the same faith which should afterwards be revealed;" that by it their transgressions may be forgiven, and then not again be committed, by God's assisting grace. *On Nature and Grace* 13.

4. The gospel has authority above heretical discussions.

459. But this may be confidently affirmed, that what took place was exactly as we are told in the Gospel narrative, and that what the wisdom of God determined upon was exactly what ought to have happened. We place the authority of the Gospel above all heretical discussions; and we admire the counsel of divine wisdom more than any counsel of any creature. *Reply to Faustus the Manichaean* 26.7.

V. The witness and help of others in salvation

A. The benefits of the prayers and witness of others

1. Prayer for another's salvation is in accord with sovereign predestination.

460. Moreover, we are admonished that the beginning of men's faith is God's gift, since the apostle signifies this when, in the Epistle to the Colossians, he says, "Continue in prayer, and watch in the same in giving of thanks. Withal praying also for us that God would open unto us the door of His word, to speak the mystery of Christ, for which also I am in bonds, that I may so make it manifest as I ought to speak." How is the door of His word opened, except when the sense of the hearer is opened so that he may believe, and, having made a beginning of faith, may admit those things which are declared and reasoned, for the purpose of building up wholesome doctrine, lest, by a heart closed through unbelief, he reject and repel those things which are spoken? *On the Predestination of the Saints* 40.

2. The prayer of his mother was answered.

461. And Thou sendest Thine hand from above, and drewest my soul out of that profound darkness, when my mother, Thy faithful one, wept to thee on my behalf more than mothers are wont to weep the bodily deaths of their children. For she saw that I was dead by that faith and spirit which she had from Thee, and Thou heardest her, O Lord. Thou heardest her, and despisedst not her tears, when, pouring down, they watered the earth under her eyes in every place where she prayed; yea, Thou heardest her. *Confessions* 3.11.

3. God works through the church.

462. Thou sawest, O Lord, how at one time, while yet a boy, being suddenly seized with pains in the stomach, and being at the point of death—Thou sawest, O my God, for even then Thou wast my keeper, with what emotion of mind and with what faith I solicited from the piety of my mother, and of Thy Church, the mother of us all, the baptism of Thy Christ, my Lord and my God. On which, the mother of my flesh being much troubled—since she, with a heart pure in Thy faith, travailed in birth more lovingly for my eternal salvation,— would, had I not quickly recovered, have without delay provided for my initiation and washing by Thy life-giving sacraments, confessing Thee, O Lord Jesus, for the remission of sins. *Confessions* 1.11.

4. Ambrose helped Augustine.

463. And to Milan I came, unto Ambrose the bishop, known to the whole world as among the best of men, Thy devout servant; whose eloquent discourse did at that time strenuously dispense unto Thy people the flour of Thy wheat, the "gladness" of Thy "oil," and the sober intoxication of Thy "wine." To him was I unknowingly led by Thee, that by him I might knowingly be led to Thee. That man of God received me like a father, and looked with a benevolent and episcopal kindliness on my change of abode. *Confessions* 5.13.

B. The relation of works and salvation

1. Daily prayer satisfied daily sins.

464. Now the daily prayer of the believer makes satisfaction for those daily sins of a momentary and trivial kind which are necessary incidents of this life. *Enchiridion* 71.

2. Almsgiving propitiated past sins.

465. We must beware, however, lest any one should suppose that gross sins, such as are committed by those who shall not inherit the kingdom of God, may be daily perpetrated, and daily atoned for by almsgiving. The life must be changed for the better; and almsgiving must be used to propitiate God for past sins, not to purchase impunity for the commission of such sins in the future. For He has given no man license to sin, although in His mercy He may blot out sins that are already committed, if we do not neglect to make proper satisfaction. *Enchiridion* 70.

3. Services for the dead are beneficial.

466. Nor can it be denied that the souls of the dead are benefited by the piety of their living friends, who offer the sacrifice of the Mediator, or give alms in the church on their behalf. But these services are of advantage only to those who during their lives have earned such merit, that services of this kind can help them. For there is a manner of life which is neither so good as not to require these services after death, nor so bad that such services are of no avail after death; there is, on the other hand, a kind of life so good as not to require them; and again, one so bad that when life is over they render no help. Therefore, it is in this life that all the merit or demerit is acquired, which can either relieve or aggravate a man's suffering after this life. No one, then, need hope that after he is dead he shall obtain merit with God which he has neglected to secure here. And accordingly it is plain that the services which the church celebrates for the dead are in no way opposed to the apostle's words: "For we must all appear before the judgment-seat of Christ; that every one may receive the things done in his body, according to that he hath done, whether it be good or bad;" for the merit which renders such services as I speak of profitable to a man, is earned while he lives in the body. It is not to every one that these services are profitable. *Enchiridion* 110.

C. Relation of baptism and forgiveness of sins

1. The meaning of baptism is death to sin, life in the Spirit.

467. And this is the meaning of the great sacrament of baptism which is solemnized among us, that all who attain to this grace should die to sin, as He is said to have died to sin, because He died in the flesh, which is the likeness of sin; and rising from the font regenerate, as He arose alive from the grave, should begin a new life in the Spirit, whatever may be the age of the body? *Enchiridion* 42.

468. "Who forgiveth all thine iniquities:" this is done in the sacrament of baptism. *On Forgiveness of Sins, and Baptism* 1.44.

2. Baptism embraces infants.

469. Now if infants are not embraced within this reconciliation and salvation, who wants them for the baptism of Christ? But if they are embraced, then are they reckoned as among the dead for whom He died; nor can they be possibly reconciled and saved by Him, unless He remit and impute not unto them their sins. *On Forgiveness of Sins, and Baptism* 1.44.

470. Whence, however, was this derived but from that primitive, as I suppose, and apostolic tradition, by which the Churches of Christ maintain it to be an inherent principle, that without baptism and partaking of the supper of the Lord it is impossible for any man to attain either to the kingdom of God or to salvation and everlasting life? So much also does Scripture testify, according to the words which we already quoted. For wherein does their opinion, who designate baptism by the term salvation, differ from what is written: "He saved us by the washing of regeneration?" or from Peter's statement: "The like figure whereunto even baptism doth also now save us?" And what else do they say who call the sacrament of the Lord's Supper life, than that which is written: "I am the living bread which came down from heaven;" and "The bread that I shall give is my flesh, for the life of the world;" and "Except ye eat the flesh of the Son of man, and drink His blood, ye shall have no life in you?" If, therefore, as so many and such divine witnesses agree, neither salvation nor eternal life can be hoped for by any man without baptism and the Lord's body and blood, it is vain to promise these blessings to infants without them. Moreover, if it be only sins that separate man from salvation and eternal life, there is nothing else in infants which these sacraments can be the means of removing, but the guilt of sin,—respecting which guilty nature it is written, that "no one is clean, not even if his life be only that of a day." *On Forgiveness of Sins, and Baptism* 1.34.

3. Baptism excludes no one.

471. For from the infant newly born to the old man bent with age, as there is none shut out from baptism, so there is none who in baptism does not die to sin. But infants die only to original sin; those who are older die also to all the sins which their evil lives have added to the sin which they brought with them. *Enchiridion* 43.

4. Baptism is not absolutely necessary.

472. For whatever unbaptized persons die confessing Christ, this confession is of the same efficacy for the remission of sins as if they were washed in the sacred font of baptism. *City of God* 13.7.

7

Free Will and Grace

I. The nature of free will

A. Free will *is first defined.*

473. Sinning therefore takes place only by exercise of will. But our will is very well known to us; for neither should I know that I will, if I did not know what will itself is accordingly, it is thus defined: will is a movement of mind, no one compelling, either for not losing or for obtaining something. *Two Souls, Against the Manichaeans* 10.14.

B. *Free will is a created good.*

474. The good will, then is a work of God, since man was created by God with a good will. On the contrary, the first bad will, which was present in man before any of his bad deeds, was rather a falling away from the work of God into man's own works than a positive work itself; in fact, a fall into bad works, since they were "according to man" and not "according to God." Thus, this bad will or, what is the same, man in so far as his will is bad is like a bad tree which brings forth these bad works like bad fruit. *City of God* 14.11.

475. God judged that men would serve him better if they served him freely. That could not be if they served him by necessity and not by free will. *Of True Religion* 14. TR

C. *Free will implies the ability to do evil.*

476. Now, the person who talks of a man making his own will evil must ask why the man made his will evil, whether because he is a nature or because he is nature made out of nothing? He will learn that the evil arises not from the fact that the man is a nature, but from the fact that the nature was made out of nothing.

For, if a nature is the cause of an evil will, then we are compelled to say that evil springs from good and that good is the cause of evil—since a bad will comes from a good nature. But how can it come about that a good, though mutable, nature, even before its will is evil, can produce something evil, namely, this evil will itself? *City of God* 12.6.

D. *Free will entails moral responsibility.*

477. If the defect we call sin overtook a man against his will, like a fever, the penalty which follows the sinner and is called condemnation would rightly seem to be unjust. But in fact sin is so much a voluntary evil that it is not sin at all unless it is voluntary. . . . We must either say that no sin has been committed or confess that it has been willingly committed. . . . Lastly, if it is not by the exercise of will that we do wrong, no one at all is to be censured or warned. . . . Therefore, it is by the will that sin is committed. *Of True Religion* 14. TR

478. So, we believe, as Scripture tells us, that God created man right and, therefore, endowed with a good will, for without a good will he would not have been "right." *City of God* 14.11.

E. *Free will involves the power not to sin.*

479. Our conclusion is that our wills have power to do all that God wanted them to do and foresaw they could do. Their power, such as it is, is a real power. What they are to do they themselves will most certainly do, because God foresaw both that they could do it and that they would do it and His knowledge cannot be mistaken. *City of God* 5.9.

F. Free will involves the power to believe or not believe.

480. Free will, naturally assigned by the creator to our rational soul, is such a neutral power, as can either incline toward faith, or turn toward unbelief. *On the Spirit and the Letter* 58.

481. Since faith, then, is in our power, inasmuch as every one believes when he likes, and, when he believes, believes voluntarily. *On the Spirit and the Letter* 55.

482. Consider now whether anybody believes, if he be unwilling; or whether he believes not, if he shall have willed it. Such a position, indeed, is absurd (for what is believing but consenting to the truth of what is said? And thus consent is certainly voluntary): faith, therefore, is in our own power. . . . Nowhere . . . in Holy Scripture do we find such an assertion as, there is no volition but comes from God. And rightly, it is not so written, because it is not true; otherwise God would be the author even of sins (which Heaven forbid!). . . . *On the Spirit and the Letter* 54.

G. Free will allows one to perform free acts.

    1. Free acts are voluntary acts.

483. He [God] grudges nothing to any, for he has given to all the possibility to be good, and has given to all the power to abide in the good as far as they would or could. *Of True Religion* 4. TR

484. In fact, sin is so much a voluntary evil that it is not sin at all unless it is voluntary. *Of True Religion* 14. TR

485. Our stand against such bold and impious attacks on God is to say that God knows all things before they happen; yet, we act by choice in all those things where we feel and know that we cannot act otherwise than willingly. *City of God* 5.9.

486. From this we conclude that the only efficient causes of all things are voluntary causes, that is to say, causes of the same nature as the spirit or breath of life. . . . The Spirit of Life, which gives life to all and is the Creator of all matter and of every created spirit is God, a Spirit, indeed, but uncreated. *City of God* 5.9.

2. Free acts are self-determined acts.

487. What cause of willing can there be which is prior to willing? Either it is a will, in which case we have not got beyond the root of evil will. Or it is not a will, and in that case there is no sin in it. Either then, will is itself the first cause of sin, or the first cause is without sin. *On Free Will* 3.49.

488. If one seeks for the efficient cause of their evil will, none is to be found. For, what can make the will bad when it is the will itself which makes an action bad? Thus, an evil will is the efficient cause of a bad action, but there is no efficient cause of an evil will. If there is such a cause, it either has or has not a will. If it has, then that will is either good or bad. If good, one would have to be foolish enough to conclude that a good will makes a bad will. In that case, a good will becomes the cause of sin—which is utterly absurd. On the other hand, if the hypothetical cause of a bad will has itself a bad will, I would have to ask what made this will bad, and, to put an end to the inquiry: What made the first bad will bad? Now, the fact is that there was no first bad will that was made bad by any other bad will—it was made bad by itself. For, if it were preceded by a cause that made it evil, that cause came first. But, if I am told that nothing made the will evil but that it always was so, then I ask whether or not it existed in some nature. *City of God* 12.6.

489. But who can fail to see that a man's coming or not coming is by the determination of his will? This determination, however, may stand alone, if the man does not come; but if he does come, it cannot be without assistance; and such assistance, that he not only knows what it is he ought to do, but also actually does what he thus knows. *On the Grace of Christ* 15.

490. A man cannot be said to have even that will with which he believes in God, without having received it . . . , but yet not so as to take away from the free will, for the good or the evil use of which they may be most righteously judged. *On the Spirit and the Letter* 58.

3. No act can be sinful unless it is free.

491. Sin is indeed nowhere but in the will, since this consideration also would have helped me, that justice holds guilty those sinning by evil will alone, although they may have been unable to accomplish what they willed. *Two Souls, Against the Manichaeans* 10.12.

492. In my *Retractations* I have this to say by way of explanation: "The Pelagians may think that this was said in their interest, on account of young children whose sin which is remitted to them in baptism they deny on the ground that they do not yet use the power of will. As if indeed the sin, which we say they derive originally from Adam, that is, that they are implicated in his guilt and on this account are held obnoxious to punishment, could ever be otherwise than in will, by which will it was committed when the transgression of the divine precept was accomplished. . . . But sin, which is never but in will, must especially be known as that which is followed by just condemnation. For this through one man entered into the world; although that sin also by which consent is yielded to concupiscence is not committed but by will." Where also in another place I have said: "Not therefore except by will is sin committed." *Two Souls, Against the Manichaeans* 10.12.

493. Sinning therefore takes place only by exercise of will. But our will is very well known to us; for neither should I know that I will, if I did not know what will itself is. Accordingly, it is thus defined: will is a movement of mind, no one compelling, either for not losing or for obtaining something. Why therefore could not I have so defined it then? Was it difficult to see that one unwilling is contrary to one willing, just as the left hand is contrary to the right, not as black to white? *Two Souls, Against the Manichaeans* 10.14.

4. Compulsion nullifies a free act.

494. I should have asked, if some stronger person had done some evil thing by the hand of one not sleeping but conscious, yet with the rest of his members bound and in constraint, whether because he knew it, though absolutely unwilling, he should be held guilty of any sin? And here all marvelling that I should ask such questions, would reply without hesitation, that he had absolutely not sinned at all. Why so? Because whoever has done anything evil by means of one unconscious or unable to resist, the latter can by no means be justly condemned. *Two Souls, Against the Manichaeans* 10.12.

495. For every one also who does a thing unwillingly is compelled, and every one who is compelled, if he does a thing, does it only unwillingly. It follows that he that is willing is free from compulsion, even if any one thinks himself compelled. And in this manner every one who willingly does a thing is not compelled, and whoever is not compelled, either does it willingly or not at all. Since nature itself proclaims these things in all men whom we can interrogate without absurdity, from the boy even to the old man, from literary sport even to the throne of the wise, why then should I not have seen that in the definition of will should be put, "no one compelling," which now as if with greater experience most cautiously I have done. . . . Hence if all these things are clearer than day, as they are, nor are they given to my conception alone, but by the liberality of truth itself to the whole human race, why could I not have said even at that time: Will is a movement of the mind, no one compelling, either for not losing or for obtaining something? *Two Souls, Against the Manichaeans* 10.14.

II. Free will and the fall

A. *Sin arises when the will chooses a lower good (see 625).*

496. The will which cleaves to the unchangeable good that is common to all, obtains man's first and best good things though it is itself only an intermediate good. But the will which turns from the unchangeable and common good and turns to its own private good or to anything exterior or inferior, sins. *On Free Will* 2.53.

497. But if the mind, being immediately conscious of itself, takes pleasure in itself to the extent of perversely imitating God, wanting to enjoy its own power, the greater it wants to be the less it becomes. Pride is the beginning of all sin. . . . To the devil's pride was added malevolent envy, so that he persuaded man to show the same pride as had proved the devil's damnation. *On Free Will* 3.76.

B. *Man fell voluntarily, without compulsion.*

   1. Sin is a free act.

498. Sinning therefore takes place only by exercise of will. *Two Souls, Against the Manichaeans* 10.14.

   2. Man sins only by will, not by compulsion.

499. This was said that by this definition a willing person might be distinguished from one not willing, and so the intention might be referred to those who first in Paradise were the origin of evil to the human race, by sinning no one compelling, that is by sinning with free will, because also knowingly they sinned against the command, and the tempters persuaded, did not compel, that this should be done. For he who ignorantly sinned may not incongruously be said to have sinned unwillingly, although not knowing what he did, yet willingly he did it. So not even the sin of such a one could be without will, which will assuredly, as it has been defined, was a "movement of the mind, no one compelling, either for not losing or for obtaining something." For he was not compelled to do what if he had been unwilling he would not have done. Because he willed, therefore he did it, even if he did not sin because he willed, being ignorant that what he did is sin. So not even such a sin could be without will, but by will of deed not by will of sin, which deed was yet sin; for this deed is what ought not to have taken place. But whoever knowingly sins, if he can without sin resist the one compelling him to sin, yet resists not, assuredly sins willingly. For he who can resist is not compelled to yield. But he who cannot by good will resist cogent covetousness, and therefore does what is contrary to the precepts of righteousness, this now is sin in the sense of being the penalty of sin. Wherefore it is most true that sin cannot be apart from will. *Retractations* 1.14.

500. God indeed, the author of nature, and certainly not of vices, created man upright; but he, being by his own will depraved, and justly condemned, begot depraved and condemned offspring. *City of God* 13.14.

C. Fallen men have lost the freedom to do good without God's help.

501. The former immortality man lost through the exercise of his free-will; the latter he shall obtain through grace, whereas, if he had not sinned, he should have obtained it by desert. . . . Just as it is in man's power to die whenever he will but the mere will cannot preserve life in the absence of food and the other means of life; so man in paradise was able of his mere will, simply by abandoning righteousness, to destroy himself; but to have maintained a life of righteousness would have been too much for his will, unless it had been sustained by the Creator's power. *Enchiridion* 106.

502. For the soul of the first man did, before the entrance of sin, govern his body with perfect freedom of will, although that body was not yet spiritual, but animal; but after the entrance of sin, that is, after sin had been committed in that flesh from which sinful flesh was thenceforward to be propagated, the reasonable soul is so appointed to occupy an inferior body, that it does not govern its body with absolute freedom of will. *Letters* 143.6.

503. And as it is certainly true, what kind of liberty, I ask, can the bond-slave possess, except when it pleases him to sin? For he is freely in bondage who does with pleasure the will of his master. Accordingly, he who is the servant of sin is free to sin. And hence he will not be free to do right, until, being freed from sin, he shall begin to be the servant of righteousness. And this is true liberty, for he has pleasure in the righteous deed; and it is at the same time a holy bondage, for he is obedient to the will of God. *Enchiridion* 30.

504. For what good work can a lost man perform, except so far as he has been delivered from perdition? Can they do anything by the free determination of their own will? Again I say, God forbid. For it was by the evil use of his free-will that man destroyed both it and himself. For, as a man who kills himself must, of course, be alive when he kills himself, but after he has killed himself ceases to live, and cannot restore himself to life; so, when man by his own free-will sinned, then sin being victorious over him, the freedom of his will was lost. *Enchiridion* 30.

D. Fallen men retain free will to do evil.

505. It is true, indeed, that the human will resides in a nature that was created good because its Creator is good, but that nature is mutable even though its Maker is immutable, for the simple reason that it was made out of nothing. Therefore, when the will turns from the good and does evil, it does so by the freedom of its own choice, but when it turns from evil and does good, it does so only with the help of God. *City of God* 15.21.

506. Thou hast made all natures and substances, which are not what Thou Thyself art, and yet they are; and that only is not from Thee which is not, and the motion of the will from Thee who art, to that which in a less degree is, because such motion is guilt and sin; and that no one's sin doth either hurt Thee, or disturb the order of Thy rule, either first or last. *Confessions* 12.11.

507. Now for the commission of sin we get no help from God; but we are not able to do justly, and to fulfil the law of righteousness in every part thereof, except we are helped by God. For as the bodily eye is not helped by the light to turn away therefrom shut or averted, but is helped by it to see, and cannot see at all unless it help it; so God, who is the light of the inner man, helps our mental sight, in order that we may do some good, not according to our own, but according to His righteousness. But if we turn away from Him, it is our own act; we then are wise according to the flesh, we then consent to the concupiscence of the flesh for unlawful deeds. When we turn to Him, therefore, God helps us; when we turn away from Him, He forsakes us. But then He helps us even to turn to Him; and this, certainly, is something that light does not do for the eyes of the body. When, therefore, He commands us in the words, "Turn ye unto me, and I will turn unto you," and we say to Him, "Turn us, O God of our salvation," and again, "Turn us, O God of hosts;" what else do we say than, "Give what Thou commandest?" *On Forgiveness of Sins, and Baptism* 2.5.

E. Fallen men retain freedom to accept God's grace.

508. As far, then, as lay in our power, we have used our influence with them, as both your brethren and our own, with a view to their persevering in the soundness of the catholic faith, which neither denies free will whether for an evil or a good life, nor attributes to it so much power that it can avail anything without God's grace, whether that it may be changed from evil to good, or that it may persevere in the pursuit of good, or that it may attain to eternal good when there is no further fear of failure. *Letters* 215.4.

509. God is said to be *"our Helper;"* but nobody can be *helped* who does not make some effort of his own accord. For God does not work our salvation in us as if he were working in insensate stones, or in creatures in whom nature has placed neither reason nor will. Why, however, He helps one man, but not another; or why one man so much, and another so much; or why one man in one way, and another in another,—He reserves to Himself according to the method of His own most secret justice, and to the excellency of His power. *On Forgiveness of Sins, and Baptism* 2.6.

510. "Keep thyself continent"? He also explained the power of the will in this matter when He said, "Having no necessity, but possessing power over his own will, to keep his virgin." And yet "all men do not receive this saying, except those to whom the power is given." Now they to whom this is not given either are unwilling or do not fulfil what they will; whereas they to whom it is given so will as to accomplish what they will. In order, therefore, that this saying, which is not received by all men, may yet be received by some, there are both the gift of God and free will. *On Grace and Free Will* 7.

III. The need for grace to aid free will

A. *All evil comes from an evil will.*

511. "Now, inasmuch as he has from God alone the capacity of being any thing at all, and of being human, why should there not be also attributed to God whatever there is in him of a good will, which could not exist unless he existed in whom it is?" But in this same manner it may also be said that a bad will also may be attributed to God as its author; because even it could not exist in man unless he were a man in whom it existed; but God is the author of his existence as man; and thus also of his bad will, which could have no existence if it had not a man in whom it might exist. But to argue thus is blasphemy. *On Forgiveness of Sins, and Baptism* 2.29.

512. As He is the Creator of all natures, so is He the giver of all powers—though He is not the maker of all choices. Evil choices are not from Him, for they are contrary to the nature which is from Him. *City of God* 5.9.

B. Grace is needed to overcome an evil will.

513. Take good heed, then, to these fearful words of the great apostle; and when you feel that you do not understand, put your faith in the meanwhile in the inspired word of God, and believe both that man's will is free, and that there is also God's grace, without whose help man's free will can neither be turned towards God, nor make any progress in God. And what you piously believe, that pray that you may have a wise understanding of. And, indeed, it is for this very purpose,—that is, that we may have a wise understanding, that there is a free will. For unless we understood and were wise with a free will, it would not be enjoined to us in the words of Scripture, "Understand now, ye simple among the people; and ye fools, at length be wise." The very precept and injunction which calls on us to be intelligent and wise, requires also our obedience; and we could exercise no obedience without free will. But if it were in our power to obey this precept to be understanding and wise by free will, without the help of God's grace, it would be unnecessary to say to God, "Give me understanding, that I may learn Thy command- ments;" nor would it have been written in the gospel, "Then opened He their understanding, that they might understand the Scriptures;" nor should the Apostle James address us in such words as, "If any of you lack wisdom, let him ask of God, who giveth to all men liberally, and upbraideth not; and it shall be given him." *Letters* 214.7.

514. For the violence with which present things acquire sway over our weakness is exactly proportioned to the superior value by which future things command our love. And oh that those who have learned to observe and bewail this may succeed in overcoming and escaping from this power of terrestrial things! Such victory and emancipation cannot, without God's grace, be achieved by the human will, which is by no means to be called free so long as it is subject to prevailing and enslaving lusts; "For of whom a man is overcome, of the same is he brought in bondage." And the Son of God has Himself said, "If the Son shall make you free, ye shall be free indeed." *Letters* 145.2.

515. Pray, therefore, for us that we may be righteous,—an attainment wholly beyond a man's reach, unless he know righteousness and be willing to practise it, but one which is immediately realized when he is perfectly willing; but this full consent of his will can never be in him unless he is healed and assisted by the grace of God. *Letters* 145.8.

C. Only the redeemed are truly free.

516. Take the case of the will. Its choice is truly free only when it is not a slave to sin and vice. God created man such a free will, but once that kind of freedom was lost by man's fall from freedom, it could be given back only by Him who had the power to give it. Thus, Truth tells us: "If therefore the Son makes you free, you will be free indeed." *City of God* 14.11.

517. Well, now, whoever you are that have said all this, what you say is by no means true; by no means, I repeat; you are much deceived, or you aim at deceiving others. We do not deny free will; but, even as the Truth declares, "if the Son shall make you free, then shall ye be free indeed." *On Marriage and Concupiscence* 1.8.

518. But whence comes this liberty to do right to the man who is in bondage and sold under sin, except he be redeemed by Him who has said, "If the Son shall make you free, ye shall be free indeed?" And before this redemption is wrought in a man, when he is not yet free to do what is right, how can he talk of the freedom of his will and his good works, except he be inflated by that foolish pride of boasting which the apostle restrains when he says, "By grace are ye saved, through faith." *Enchiridion* 30.

D. Grace is needed to keep God's laws.

519. If, however, any one says that there is a free will in man for worshipping God aright, without His assistance; and whosoever says that God is the Creator of those that are born, in such wise as to deny that infants have any need of one to redeem them from the power of the devil: that is the man who is set down as a disciple of Coelestius and Pelagius. *On Marriage and Concupiscence* 1.8.

520. It follows, then, dearly beloved, beyond all doubt, that as your good life is nothing else than God's grace, so also the eternal life which is the recompense of a good life is the grace of God; moreover it is given gratuitously, even as that is given gratuitously to which it is given. *On Grace and Free Will* 20.

521. Nevertheless, this merely shows that any will, however good, would have been destitute and destined to remain in hopeless desire, did not He who had created their good nature out of nothing, and had given it a capacity for union with Himself, first awaken in the will a greater longing for this union and then fill the will with some of His very Being in order to make it better. *City of God* 12.9.

522. But even now there are some, as there were then among the Jews, of whom it is said: "Not knowing the justice of God and seeking to establish their own, they have not submitted themselves to the justice of God." No doubt they think they are justified by the Law, and that their own free will enables them to keep it. This means that their justice is derived from their own human nature, not given by divine grace, which is the reason of its being called the justice of God. *Letters* 177. FOC

E. Grace is needed to perform any good act.

523. For if nothing but this "capacity" of ours were assisted by this grace, the Lord would rather have said, "Every man that hath heard and hath learned of the Father *may possibly* come unto me." This, however, is not what He said; but His words are these: "Every man that hath heard and hath learned of the Father *cometh* unto me." Now *the possibility of coming* Pelagius places in nature, or even—as we found him attempting to say some time ago—in grace (whatever that may mean according to him),—when he says, "whereby this very capacity is assisted;" whereas *the actual coming* lies in the will and act. It does not, however, follow that he who *may* come actually comes, unless he has also willed and acted for the coming. But every one who has learned of the Father not only has the possibility of coming, but *comes;* and in this result are already included the *motion* of the capacity, the *affection* of the will, and the *effect* of the action. *On the Grace of Christ* 15.

524. For if we have from God a certain free will, which may still be either good or bad; but the good will comes from ourselves; then that which comes from ourselves is better than that which comes from Him. But inasmuch as it is the height of absurdity to say this, they ought to acknowledge that we attain from God even a good will. It would indeed be a strange thing if the will could so stand in some mean as to be neither good or bad; for we either love righteousness, and it is good, and if we love it more, more good,—if less, it is less good; or if we do not love it at all, it is not good. *On Forgiveness of Sins, and Baptism* 2.30.

F. Even faith is a gift of God.

525. And lest men should arrogate to themselves the merit of their own faith at least, not understanding that this too is the gift of God, this same apostle, who says in another place that he had "obtained mercy of the Lord to be faithful," here also adds: "and that not of yourselves; it is the gift of God: not of works, lest any man should boast." *Enchiridion* 31.

526. Such passages do they collect out of the Scriptures,—like the one which I just now quoted, "Turn ye unto me, and I will turn unto you,"—as if it were owing to the merit of our turning to God that His grace were given us, wherein He Himself even turns unto us. Now the persons who hold this opinion fail to observe that, unless our turning to God were itself God's gift, it would not be said to Him in prayer, "Turn us again, O God of hosts;" and "Thou, O God, wilt turn and quicken us;" and again, "Turn us, O God of our salvation,"—with other passages of similar import, too numerous to mention here. *On Grace and Free Will* 10.

527. His last clause runs thus: "I have kept the faith." But he who says this is the same who declares in another passage, "I have obtained mercy that I might be faithful." He does not say, "I obtained mercy because I was faithful," but "in order that I might be faithful," thus showing that even faith itself cannot be had without God's mercy, and that it is the gift of God. *On Grace and Free Will* 17.

G. *But God's gifts are received by free choice.*

1. We receive grace through prayer.

528. For "how," says he, "shall they call upon Him in whom they have not believed?" The spirit of grace, therefore, causes us to have faith, in order that through faith we may, on praying for it, obtain the ability to do what we are commanded. On this account the apostle himself constantly puts faith before the law; since we are not able to do what the law commands unless we obtain the strength to do it by the prayer of faith. *On Grace and Free Will* 28.

2. We must cooperate with God's grace.

529. Wherefore, most dearly beloved, whosoever says, My will suffices for me to perform good works, declines to the right. But, on the other hand, they who think that a good way of life should be forsaken, when they hear God's grace so preached as to lead to the supposition and belief that it of itself makes men's wills from evil to good, and it even of itself keeps them what it has made them; and who, as the result of this opinion, go on to say, "Let us do evil that good may come,"—these persons decline to the left. *Letters* 215.4.

530. "That, however, we really do a good thing, or speak a good word, or think a good thought, proceeds *both from ourselves and from Him!*" This, however, he has not said. But, if I am not mistaken, I think I see why he was afraid to do so. *On the Grace of Christ* 17.

531. Now, do the many precepts which are written in the law of God, forbidding all fornication and adultery, indicate anything else than free will? Surely such precepts would not be given unless a man had a will of his own, wherewith to obey the divine commandments. And yet it is God's gift which is indispensable for the observance of the precepts of chastity. *On Grace and Free Will* 8.

3. God helps weak but willing men.

532. He, therefore, who wishes to do God's commandment, but is unable, already possesses a good will, but as yet a small and weak one; he will, however, become able when he shall have acquired a great and robust will. *On Grace and Free Will* 33.

533. For it is certain that we keep the commandments if we will; but because the will is prepared by the Lord, we must ask of Him for such a force of will as suffices to make us act by the willing. It is certain that it is we that *will* when we will, but it is He who makes us will what is good, of whom it is said (as he has just now expressed it), "The will is prepared by the Lord." Of the same Lord it is said, "The steps of a man are ordered by the Lord, and his way doth He will." Of the same Lord again it is said, "It is God who worketh in you, even to will!" It is certain that it is we that act when we act; but it is He who makes us act, by applying efficacious powers to our will, who has said, "I will make you to walk in my statutes, and to observe my judgments, and to do them." *On Grace and Free Will* 32.

4. God prepares and perfects our wills.

534. And who was it that had begun to give him his love, however small, but He who prepares the will, and perfects by His co-operation what He initiates by His operation? Forasmuch as in beginning He works in us that we may have the will, and in perfecting works with us when we have the will. On which account the apostle says, "I am confident of this very thing, that He which hath begun a good work in you will perform it until the day of Jesus Christ." He operates, therefore, without us, in order that we may will; but when we will, and so will that we may act, He co-operates with us. We can, however, ourselves do nothing to effect good works of piety without Him either working that we may will, or co-working when we will. Now, concerning His working that we may will, it is said: "It is God which worketh in you, even to will." While of His co-working with us, when we will and act by willing, the apostle says, "We know that in all things there is co-working for good to them that love God." *On Grace and Free Will* 33.

535. Lest, however, it should be thought that men themselves in this matter do nothing by free will, it is said in the Psalm, "Harden not your hearts;" and in Ezekiel himself, "Cast away from you all your transgressions, which ye have impiously committed against me; and make you a new heart and a new spirit; and keep all my commandments. . . . We should remember that He says, "Make you a new heart and a new spirit," who also promises, "I will give you a new heart, and a new spirit will I put within you." How is it, then, that He who says, "Make you," also says, "I will give you"? Why does He command, if He is to give? Why does He give if man is to make, except it be that He gives what He commands when He Helps him to obey whom He commands? . . . By it also it comes to pass that the very good will, which has now begun to be, is enlarged, and made so great that it is able to fulfil the divine commandments which it shall wish, when it shall once firmly and perfectly wish. This is the purport of what the Scripture says: "If thou wilt, thou shalt keep the commandments." *On Grace and Free Will* 31.

H. However, there is no merit in our free will.

536. And further, should any one be inclined to boast, not indeed of his works, but of the freedom of his will, as if the first merit belonged to him, this very liberty of good action being given to him as a reward he had earned, let him listen to this same preacher of grace, when he says: "For it is God which worketh in you, both to will and to do of His own good pleasure." *Enchiridion* 32.

537. Men, however, are laboring to find in our own will some good thing of our own,—not given to us by God; but how it is to be found I cannot imagine. The apostle says, when speaking of men's good works, "What hast thou that thou didst not receive? now, if thou didst receive it, why dost thou glory, as if thou hadst not received it?" But, besides this, even reason itself, which may be estimated in such things by such as we are, sharply restrains every one of us in our investigations so as that we may not so defend grace as to seem to take away free will, or, on the other hand, so assert free will as to be judged ungrateful to the grace of God, in our arrogant impiety. *On Forgiveness of Sins, and Baptism* 2.28.

538. Nor can we possibly, without extreme absurdity, maintain that there previously existed in any man the good merit of a good will, to entitle him to the removal of his stony heart, when all the while this very heart of stone signifies nothing else than a will of the hardest kind and such as is absolutely inflexible against God? *On Grace and Free Will* 29.

539. But they who maintain that God's grace is given according to our merits, receive these testimonies of Scripture in such a manner as to believe that our merit lies in the circumstance of our "being with God," while His grace is given according to this merit, so that He too may be with us. In like manner, that our merit lies in the fact of "our seeking God," and then His grace is given according to this merit, in order that we may find Him. *On Grace and Free Will* 11.

IV. The nature and function of grace with free will

A. **God's grace is necessary for our free will (see 511–539).**

B. **God's grace is prevenient (prior) to our free choice.**

540. But it was because they had been chosen, that they chose Him; not because they chose Him that they were chosen. There could be no merit in men's choice of Christ, if it were not that God's grace was prevenient in His choosing them. *On Grace and Free Will* 38.

C. **God's grace works in cooperation with our free choice (see 529–531).**

D. **God's grace is effectual on our wills.**

541. We read in Holy Scripture, both that God's mercy "shall meet me," and that His mercy "shall follow me." It goes before the unwilling to make him willing; it follows the willing to make his will effectual. *Enchiridion* 32.

E. **God's will is necessarily accomplished by our wills.**

542. For, as far as they were concerned, they did what God did not will that they do, but as far as God's omnipotence is concerned, they were quite unable to achieve their purpose. In the very act of going against his will, his will was thereby accomplished. . . . Actually, God achieveth some of his purposes—which are, of course, all good—through the evil wills of bad men. *Enchiridion* 26.

F. God's grace works mysteriously and ineffably on man's free will.

543. Now if God is able, either through the agency of angels (whether good ones or evil), or in any other way whatever, to operate in the hearts even of the wicked, in return for their deserts,—whose wickedness was not made by Him, but was either derived originally from Adam, or increased by their own will,—what is there to wonder at if, through the Holy Spirit, He works good in the hearts of the elect, who has wrought it that their hearts become good instead of evil? *On Grace and Free Will* 43.

544. Therefore read and understand, observe and acknowledge, that it is not by law and teaching uttering their lessons from without, but by a secret, wonderful, and ineffable power operating within, that God works in men's hearts not only revelations of the truth, but also good dispositions of the will. *On the Grace of Christ* 25.

V. Some problems in man's understanding of grace and free will

A. Why did God create men He knew would sin?

545. Here we have an answer to the problem why God should have created men whom He foresaw would sin. It was because both in them and by means of them He could reveal how much was deserved by their guilt and condoned by His grace, and, also, because the harmony of the whole of reality which verse discordancy of those who sin. *City of God* 14.26.

B. What is the relation between foreknowledge and free will?

546. Wherefore, God would have been willing to preserve even the first man in that state of salvation in which he was created, and after he had begotten sons to remove him at a fit time, without the intervention of death, to a better place, where he should have been not only free from sin, but free even from the desire of sinning, if He had foreseen that man would have the steadfast will to persist in the state of innocence in which he was created. But as He foresaw that man would make a bad use of his free-will, that is, would sin, God arranged His own designs rather with a view to do good to man even in his sinfulness, that thus the good will of the Omnipotent might not be made void by the evil will of man, but might be fulfilled in spite of it. *Enchiridion* 104.

547. So with us, when we say we *must* choose freely when we choose at all, what we say is true; yet, we do not subject free choice to any necessity which destroys our liberty. Our choices, therefore, are our own, and they effect, whenever we choose to act, something that would not happen if we had not chosen. *City of God* 5.10.

548. The conclusion is that we are by no means under compulsion to abandon free choice in favor of divine foreknowledge, nor need we deny—God forbid!—that God knows the future, as a condition for holding free choice. *City of God* 5.10.

C. Does God desire all men to be saved?

1. Earlier Augustine: Yes.

549. If we believe that we may attain this grace (and of course believe voluntarily), then the question arises, whence we have this will?—if from nature, why it is not at everybody's command, since the same God made all men? if from God's gift, then again, why is not the gift open to all, since "He will have all men to be saved, and to come unto the knowledge of the truth? . . ." God no doubt wishes all men to be saved and to come into the knowledge of the truth; but yet not so as to take away from them free will, for the good or the evil use of which they may be most righteously judged. *On the Spirit and the Letter* 57,58.

2. Later Augustine: No.

550. Accordingly, when we hear and read in Scripture that He "will have all men to be saved," although we know well that all men are not saved, we are not on that account to restrict the omnipotence of God, but are rather to understand the Scripture, "Who will have all men to be saved," as meaning that no man is saved unless God wills his salvation: not that there is no man whose salvation He does not will, but that no man is saved apart from His will; and that, therefore, we should pray Him to will our salvation, because if He will it, it must necessarily be accomplished. *Enchiridion* 103.

551. Our Lord says plainly, however, in the Gospel, when upbraiding the impious city: "How often would I have gathered thy children together, even as a hen gathereth her chickens under her wings, and ye would not!" as if the will of God had been overcome by the will of men, . . . But even though she was unwilling, He gathered together as many of her children as He wished: for He does not will some things and do them, and will others and do them not; but "He hath done all that He pleased in heaven and in earth." *Enchiridion* 97.

552. And on the same principle we interpret the expression in the Gospel: "The true light which lighteth every man that cometh into the world;" not that there is no man who is not enlightened, but that no man is enlightened except by Him. *Enchiridion* 103.

D. Will the redeemed be free in heaven?

553. The souls in bliss will still possess the freedom of will, though sin will have no power to tempt them. They will be more free than ever—so free, in fact, from all delight in sinning as to find, in not sinning, an unfailing source of joy. . . . Freedom is that more potent freedom which makes all sin impossible. *City of God* 22.30.

554. Now it was expedient that man should be at first so created, as to have it in his power both to will what was right and to will what was wrong; not without reward if he willed the former, and not without punishment if he willed the latter. But in the future life it shall not be in his power to will evil; and yet this will constitute no restriction on the freedom of his will. On the contrary, his will shall be much freer when it shall be wholly impossible for him to be the slave of sin. We should never think of blaming the will, or saying that it was no will, or that it was not to be called free, when we so desire happiness, that not only do we shrink from misery, but find it utterly impossible to do otherwise. As, then, the soul even now finds it impossible to desire unhappiness, so in future it shall be wholly impossible for it to desire sin. But God's arrangement was not to be broken, according to which He willed to show how good is a rational being who is able even to refrain from sin, and yet how much better is one who cannot sin at all. *Enchiridion* 105.

E. Is God's saving grace resistible?

1. Earlier Augustine: Yes.

555. For the soul cannot receive and possess these gifts, which are here referred to, except by yielding its consent. And thus whatever it possess, and whatever it receives, is from God; and yet the act of receiving and having belongs, of course, to the receiver and possessor. *On the Spirit and the Letter* 60.

556. To yield our consent, indeed, to God's summons, or to withhold it, is (as I have said) the function of our will. *On the Spirit and the Letter* 60.

557. This being the case, unbelievers indeed do contrary to the will of God when they do not believe the gospel; nevertheless they do not therefore overcome His will, but rob their own selves of the great, nay the very greatest, good, and implicate themselves in penalties of punishment. . . . Thus God's will is for ever invincible. *On the Spirit and the Letter* 58.

2. Later Augustine: No.

558. And, moreover, who will be so foolish and blasphemous as to say that God cannot change the evil wills of men, whichever, whenever, and wheresoever He chooses, and direct them to what is good? But when He does this, He does it of mercy; when He does it not, it is of justice that He does it not; for "He hath mercy on whom He will have mercy, and whom He will He hardeneth." *Enchiridion* 98.

559. We read in Holy Scripture, both that God's mercy "shall meet me," and that His mercy "shall follow me." It goes before the unwilling to make him willing; it follows the willing to make his will effectual. Why are we taught to pray for our enemies, who are plainly unwilling to lead a holy life, unless that God may work willingness in them? And why are we ourselves taught to ask that we may receive, unless that He who has created in us the wish, may Himself satisfy the wish? We pray, then, for our enemies, that the mercy of God may prevent them, as it has prevented us: we pray for ourselves that His mercy may follow us. *Enchiridion* 32.

560. Great indeed is the help of the grace of God, so that He turns our heart in whatever direction He pleases. But according to this writer's foolish opinion, however great the help may be, we deserve it all at the moment when, without any assistance beyond the liberty of our will, we hasten to the Lord, desire His guidance and direction, suspend our own will entirely on His, and by close adherence to Him become one spirit with Him. Now all these vast courses of goodness we (according to him) accomplish, forsooth, simply by the freedom of our own free will; and by reason of such antecedent merits we so secure His grace, that He turns our heart which way soever He pleases. *On the Grace of Christ* 24.

F. Is God's saving grace compulsive?

   1. Earlier Augustine: No (see 476–494).

561. Nor are we dismayed by the difficulty that what we choose to do freely is done of necessity, because He whose foreknowledge cannot be deceived foreknew that we would choose to do it. This was the fear that made Cicero oppose foreknowledge. *City of God* 5.9.

562. However, our main point is that, from the fact that to God the order of all causes is certain, there is no logical deduction that there is no power in the choice of our will. The fact is that our choices fall within the order of the causes which is known for certain to God and is contained in His foreknowledge—for, human choices are the causes of human acts. It follows that He who foreknew the causes of all things could not be unaware that our choices were among those causes which were foreknown as the causes of our acts. *City of God* 5.9.

563. It does not follow, therefore, that the order of causes, known for certain though it is in the foreknowing mind of God, brings it about that there is no power in our will, since our choices themselves have an important place in the order of causes. *City of God* 5.9.

2. Later Augustine: Yes.

564. And yet, after calling Peter and the other apostles by His words alone, when He came to summon Paul, who was before called Saul, subsequently the powerful builder of His Church, but originally its cruel persecutor, He not only constrained him with His voice, but even dashed him to the earth with His power; and that He might forcibly bring one who was raging amid the darkness of infidelity to desire the light of the heart, He first struck him with physical blindness of the eyes. *Correction of the Donatists* 6.22.

565. Whence also the Lord Himself bids the guests in the first instance to be invited to His great supper, and afterwards compelled; for on His servants making answer to Him, "Lord, it is done as Thou hast commanded, and yet there is room," He said to them, "Go out into the highways and hedges, and compel them to come in." In those, therefore, who were first brought in with gentleness, the former obedience is fulfilled; but in those who were compelled, the disobedience is avenged. *Correction of the Donatists* 6.24.

566. Where is what the Donatists were wont to cry: Man is at liberty to believe or not believe? Towards whom did Christ use violence? Whom did He compel? Here they have the Apostle Paul. Let them recognize in his case Christ first compelling, and afterwards teaching; first striking, and afterwards consoling. For it is wonderful how he who entered the service of the gospel in the first instance under the compulsion of bodily punishment, afterwards labored more in the gospel than all they who were called by word only; and he who was compelled by the greater influence of fear to love, displayed that perfect love which casts our fear.

Why, therefore, should not the Church use force in compelling her lost sons to return, if the lost sons compelled others to their destruction? *Correction of the Donatists* 6.22,23.

567. Wherefore, if the power which the Church has received by divine appointment in its due season, through the religious character and the faith of kings, be the instrument by which those who are found in the highways and hedges—that is, in heresies and schisms—are compelled to come in, then let them not find fault with being compelled, but consider whether they be so compelled. The supper of the Lord is the unity of the body of Christ, not only in the sacrament of the altar, but also in the bond of peace. Of the Donatists themselves, indeed, we can say that they compel no man to any good thing; for whomsoever they compel, they compel to nothing else but evil. *Correction of the Donatists* 6.24.

G. Why is it just to save only some?

1. Earlier Augustine: Because God had foreknowledge of who would believe.

568. There was justice in instituting rewards and punishments for good and wicked deeds. For, no one sins because God foreknew that he would sin. In fact, the very reason why a man is undoubtedly responsible for his own sin, when he sins, is because He whose foreknowledge cannot be deceived foresaw, not the man's fate or fortune or what not, but that the man himself would be responsible for his own sin. No man sins unless it is his choice to sin; and his choice not to sin, that, too, God foresaw. *City of God* 5.10.

2. Later Augustine: Because all men deserve hell.

569. For then he perceives that the whole human race was condemned in its rebellious head by a divine judgment so just, that if not a single member of the race had been redeemed, no one could justly have questioned the justice of God; and that it was right that those who are redeemed should be redeemed in such a way as to show, by the greater number who are unredeemed and left in their just condemnation, what the whole race deserved, and whither the deserved judgment of God would lead even the redeemed, did not His undeserved mercy interpose, so that every mouth might be stopped of those who wish to glory in their own merits, and that he that glorieth might glory in the Lord. *Enchiridion* 99.

570. Furthermore, who would be so impiously foolish as to say that God cannot turn the evil wills of men—as he willeth, when he willeth, and where he willeth—toward the good? But when he acteth, he acteth through mercy; when he doth not act, it is through justice. *Enchiridion* 98.

571. As the Supreme Good, he made good use of evil deeds, for the damnation of those whom he had justly predestined to punishment and for the salvation of those whom he had mercifully predestined to grace. *Enchiridion* 100.

H. Is it fair to condemn infants who have made no free choice?

   1. All men are born sinners.

572. They [infants] are held guilty not by propriety of will but of origin. For what is every earthly man in origin but Adam. *Retractations* 1.14.

573. But what can be plainer than the many weighty testimonies of the divine declarations, which afford to us the clearest proof possible that without union with Christ there is no man who can attain to eternal life and salvation; and that no man can unjustly be damned,—that is, separated from that life and salvation,—by the judgment of God? The inevitable conclusion from these truths is this, that, as nothing else is effected when infants are baptized except that they are incorporated into the church, in other words, that they are united with the body and members of Christ, unless this benefit has been bestowed upon them, they are manifestly in danger of damnation. Damned, however, they could not be if they really had no sin. Now, since their tender age could not possibly have contracted sin in its own life, it remains for us, even if we are as yet unable to understand, at least to believe that infants inherit original sin. *On Forgiveness of Sins, and Baptism* 3.7.

   2. Infants can be regenerated through baptism.

574. They, therefore, who say that the reason why infants are baptized, is, that they may have the remission of the sin which they have themselves committed in their life, not what they have derived from Adam, may be refuted without much difficulty. *On Forgiveness of Sins, and Baptism* 1.22.

575. They also say that little children do not have to be baptized to secure salvation, and thus, by this deadly doctrine, they bring eternal death upon them by promising that even though not baptized they will have everlasting life, because they do not belong to those of whom the Lord said: "For the Son of man is come to seek and to save that which was lost." They say that infants had not been lost, that there was nothing in them requiring salvation or redemption at such a price, because there was nothing depraved in them, nothing that held them captive under the power of the Devil, and that what we read about blood shed for the remission of sins does not apply to them. *Letters* 175. FOC

3. God foreknew unbaptized infants would be ungodly.

576. You must refer the matter, then, to the hidden determinations of God, when you see, in one and the same condition, such as all infants unquestionably have,—who derive their hereditary evil from Adam,—that one is assisted so as to be baptized, and another is not assisted, so that he dies in his very bondage; and again, that one baptized person is left and forsaken in his present life, who God foreknew would be ungodly, while another baptized person is taken away from this life, "lest that wickedness should alter his understanding." *On Grace and Free Will* 41.

4. Unbaptized infants will have the least punishment in hell.

577. It may therefore be correctly affirmed, that such infants as quit the body without being baptized will be involved in the mildest condemnation of all. *On Forgiveness of Sins, and Baptism* 1.21.

5. All infants are guilty of sin in Adam.

578. The Pelagians may think that this was said in their interest, on account of young children whose sin which is remitted to them in baptism they deny on the grounds that they do not yet use the power of will. As if indeed that sin, which we say they derive originally from Adam, that is, that they are implicated in his guilt and on this account are held obnoxious to punishment, could ever be otherwise than in will by which will it was committed when the transgression of the divine precept was accomplished. *Retractations* 1.14.

579. "It is," they say, "by no means conceded that God who remits to a man his own sins imputes to him another's." He remits, indeed, but it is to those regenerated by the Spirit, not to those generated by the flesh; but He imputes to a man no longer the sins of another, but only his own. They were no doubt the sins of another, whilst as yet they were not in existence who bore them when propagated; but now the sins belong to them by carnal generation, to whom they have not yet been remitted by spiritual regeneration. *On Forgiveness of Sins, and Baptism* 3.15.

8

Evil

I. Every substance as such is good.

A. All of God's creation is good.

580. Therefore, if the world was made out of some unformed matter, that matter was made out of absolutely nothing. If it was as yet unformed, still it was at least capable of receiving form. By God's goodness it is "formable." Even capacity for form is good. The author of all good things, who gives form, also gives the capacity for form. All that exists receives existence from God, and that which does not yet exist but may do so, receives its potential existence from God. In other words, all that is formed receives its form from God, and from him all that is not yet formed receives power to be formed. Nothing has integrity of nature unless it be whole of its kind. From God comes all wholeness as every good thing comes from him. *Of True Religion* 18. TR

581. All natures, then, inasmuch as they are, and have therefore a rank and species of their own, and a kind of internal harmony, are certainly good. And when they are in the places assigned to them by the Order of their nature, they preserve such being as they have received. And those things which have not received everlasting being, are altered for better or for worse, so as to suit the wants and motions of those things to which the Creator's law has made them subservient. *City of God* 12.5.

582. How opposed this is to the meaning of this authoritative Scripture, which, in recounting all the works of God, regularly adds, "And God saw that it was good;" and, when all were completed, inserts the words, "And God saw everything that He had made, and, behold, it was very good." Was it not obviously meant to be understood that there was no other cause of the world's creation than that good creatures should be made by a good God? *City of God* 11.23.

583. For these things, as you describe them, cannot be called evil; for all such things, as far as they exist, must have their existence from the most high God, for as far as they exist they are good. If pain and weakness is an evil, the animals you speak of were of such physical strength that their abortive offspring, after, as your sect believes, the world was formed of them, fell from heaven to earth, according to you, and could not die. If blindness is an evil, they could see; if deafness, they could hear. If to be nearly or altogether dumb is an evil, their speech was so clear and intelligible, that, as you assert, they decided to make war against God in compliance with an address delivered in their assembly. If sterility is an evil, they were prolific in children. If exile is an evil, they were in their own country, and occupied their own territories. If servitude is an evil, some of them were rulers. If death is an evil, they were alive, and the life was such that, by your statement, even after God was victorious, it was impossible for the mind ever to die. *On the Morals of the Manichaeans* 9.14.

B. There is no evil substance (see 602-604).

584. No nature, therefore, as far as it is nature, is evil; but to each nature there is no evil except to be diminished in respect of good. But if by being diminished it should be consumed so that there is not good, no nature would be left; not only such as the Manichaeans introduce, where so great good things are found that their exceeding blindness is wonderful, but such as any one can introduce. *On the Nature of Good* 17.

585. Existence as such is good, and supreme existence is the chief good. From what did he make them? Out of nothing. Whatever is must have some form, and though it be but a minimal good it will be good and will be of God. The highest form is the highest good, and the lowest form is the lowest good. Every good thing is either God or derived from God. Therefore even the lowest form is of God. And the same may be said of species. We rightly praise alike that which has form and that which has species. That out of which God created all things had neither form nor species, and was simply nothing. That which by comparison with perfect things is said to be without form, but which has any form at all, however small or inchoate, is not nothing. It, too, in so far as it has any being at all, is of God. *Of True Religion* 18. TR

C. All who depart from goodness show they were created good.

586. And who can worthily conceive or express how great a glory that is, to cleave to God, so as to live to Him, to draw wisdom from Him, to delight in Him, and to enjoy this so great good, without death, error, or grief? And thus, since every vice is an injury of the nature, that very vice of the wicked angels, their departure from God, is sufficient proof that God created their nature so good, that it is an injury to it not to be with God. *City of God* 12.1.

587. And this its sin is itself proof that its nature was originally good. For had it not been very good, though not equal to its Creator, the desertion of God as its light could not have been an evil to it. For as blindness is a vice of the eye, and this very fact indicates that the eye was created to see the light, and as, consequently, vice itself proves that the eye is more excellent than the other members, because it is capable of light (for on no other supposition would it be a vice of the eye to want light), so the nature which once enjoyed God teaches, even by its very vice, that it was created the best of all, since it is now miserable because it does not enjoy God. *City of God* 22.1.

D. No departures from goodness are from God.

588. But when we hear: "All things are from Him, and through Him, and in Him," we ought assuredly to understand all natures which naturally exist. For sins, which do not preserve but vitiate nature, are not from Him; which sins, Holy Scripture in many ways testifies, are from the will of those sinning. *On the Nature of Good* 28.

589. Is the same thing then both good and evil? By no means; but evil is what is against nature, for this is evil both to the animal and to us. This evil is the disagreement, which certainly is not a substance, but hostile to substance. Whence then is it? See what it leads to, and you will learn, if any inner light lives in you. It leads all that it destroys to non-existence. Now God is the author of existence; and there is no existence which, as far as it is existing, leads to non-existence. Thus we learn whence disagreement is not; as to whence it is, nothing can be said. *On the Morals of the Manichaeans* 8.11.

II. The supreme good is incorruptible.

A. *Created good results from a good Creator.*

590. Neither is there any author more excellent than God, nor any skill more efficacious than the word of God, nor any cause better than that good might be created by the good God. This also Plato has assigned as the most sufficient reason for the creation of the world, that good works might be made by a good God; whether he read this passage, or, perhaps, was informed of these things by those who had read them, or, by his quick-sighted genius, penetrated to things spiritual and invisible through the things that are created, or was instructed regarding them by those who had discerned them. *City of God* 11.21.

B. *The supreme good is eternal and incorruptible.*

591. Since you make the kingdom of light to be God, attributing to it an uncompounded nature, so that it has no part inferior to another, you must grant, however decidedly in opposition to yourselves, you must grant, nevertheless, that this nature, which you not only do not deny to be the chief good, but spend all your strength in trying to show that it is so, is immutable, incorruptible, impenetrable, inviolable, for otherwise it should not be the chief good; for the chief good is that than which there is nothing better, and for such a nature to be hurt is impossible. Again, if, as has been shown, to hurt is to deprive of good, there can be no hurt to the kingdom of darkness, for there is no good in it. And as the kingdom of light cannot be hurt, as it is inviolable, what can the evil you speak of be hurtful to? *On the Morals of the Manichaeans* 3.5.

592. Eternal life surpasses temporal life in vivacity, and only by knowing do I get a glimpse of what eternity is. By looking at eternity with the mind's eye I remove from it all changeableness, and in eternity I see no temporal duration, for periods of time are constituted by the movements, past or future, of things. In eternity there is neither past nor future. What is past has ceased to be, and what is future has not yet begun to be. Eternity is ever the same. It never "was" in the sense that it is not now, and it never "will be" in the sense that it is not yet. Wherefore, eternity alone could have said to the human mind "I am what I am." And of eternity alone could it be truly said: "He who is hath sent me" (Ex. 3:14). *Of True Religion* 49. TR

593. But to Him to live, to understand, to be blessed, are to *be*. They have understood, from this unchangeableness and this simplicity, that all things must have been made by Him, and that He could Himself have been made by none. *City of God* 8.6.

C. The supreme good is separate from corruptible substance.

594. Now, if corruption is an evil, both incorruption and incorruptibility must be good things. We are not, however, speaking at present of incorruptible nature, but of things which admit of corruption, and which, while not corrupted, may be called incorrupt, but not incorruptible. That alone can be called incorruptible which not only is not corrupted, but also cannot in any part be corrupted. Whatever things, then, being incorrupt, but liable to corruption, begin to be corrupted, are deprived of the good which they had as incorrupt. Nor is this a slight good, for corruption is a great evil. And the continued increase of corruption implies the continued presence of good, of which they may be deprived. Accordingly, the natures supposed to exist in the region of darkness must have been either corruptible or incorruptible. If they were incorruptible, they were in possession of a good than which nothing is higher. If they were corruptible, they were either corrupted or not corrupted. If they were not corrupted, they were incorrupt, to say which of everything is to give it great praise. *Against the Epistle of Manichaeus* 35.

595. The highest essence imparts existence to all that exists. That is why it is called essence. Death imparts no actual existence to anything which has died. If it is really dead it has indubitably been reduced to nothingness. For things die only in so far as they have a decreasing part in existence. That can be more briefly put in this way: things die according as they become less. Matter is less than any kind of life, since it is life that keeps even the tiniest quantity of matter together in any thing, whether it be the life that governs any particular living thing, or that which governs the entire universe of natural things. Matter is therefore subject to death, and is thereby nearer to nothingness. Life which delights in material joys and neglects God tends to nothingness and is thereby iniquity. *Of True Religion* 11. TR

III. Only created goods are corruptible.

A. *All substance is created by God.*

596. And as to natural causes, we by no means separate them from the will of Him who is the author and framer of all nature. But now as to voluntary causes. They are referable either to God, or to angels, or to men, or to animals of whatever description, if indeed those instinctive movements of animals devoid of reason. *City of God* 5.9.

597. But "from Him" does not mean the same as "of Him." For what is of Him may be said to be from Him; but not everything that is from Him is rightly said to be of Him. For from Him are heaven and earth, because He made them; but not of Him because they are not of His substance. As in the case of a man who begets a son and makes a house, from himself is the son, from himself is the house, but the son is of him, the house is of earth and wood. But this is so, because as a man he cannot make something even of nothing; but God of whom are all things, through whom are all things, in whom are all things, had no need of any material which He had not made to assist His omnipotence. *On the Nature of Good* 27.

B. *Created goods are corruptible because they are mutable.*

598. All corruptible natures therefore are natures at all only so far as they are *from* God, nor would they be corruptible if they were *of*

him; because they would be what He himself is. Therefore of whatever order, they are, they are so because it is God by whom they were made; but they are not immutable, because it is nothing of which they were made. For it is sacrilegious audacity to make nothing and God equal, as when we wish to make what has been born of God such as what has been made by Him out of nothing. *On the Nature of Good* 10.

599. But as the sentient nature, even when it feels pain, is superior to the stony, which can feel none, so the rational nature, even when wretched, is more excellent than that which lacks reason or feeling, and can therefore experience no misery. And since this is so, then in this nature which has been created so excellent, that though it be mutable itself, it can yet secure its blessedness by adhering to the immutable good, the supreme God; and since it is not satisfied unless it be perfectly blessed, and cannot be thus blessed save in God,—in this nature, I say, not to adhere to God, is manifestly a fault. Now every fault injures the nature, and is consequently contrary to the nature. *City of God* 12.1.

C. Created goods differ in degree.

600. It remains, therefore, that you must confess that God made the region of light out of nothing; and you are unwilling to believe this; because if God could make out of nothing some great good which yet was inferior to Himself, He could also, since He is good, and grudges no good, make another good inferior to the former, and again a third inferior to the second, and so on, in order down to the lowest good of created natures, so that the whole aggregate, instead of extending indefinitely without number or measure, should have a fixed and definite consistency. *Against the Epistle of Manichaeus* 25.

D. Corruption results from abandoning uncreated good.

601. There is no need, therefore, that in our sins and vices we accuse the nature of the flesh to the injury of the Creator, for in its own kind and degree the flesh is good; but to desert the Creator good, and live according to the created good, is not good, whether a man choose to live according to the flesh, or according to the soul, or according to the whole human nature, which is composed of flesh and soul, and which is therefore spoken of either by the name flesh alone, or by the name soul alone. *City of God* 14.5.

IV. Evil is not a substance.

A. *Evil tends toward nonexistence.*

602. Now, according to you [Manichaeans], evil is a certain nature and substance. Moreover, whatever is contrary to nature must oppose nature and seek its destruction. For nature means nothing else than that which anything is conceived of as being in its own kind. Hence is the new word which we now use derived from the word for being,—essence namely, or, as we usually say, substance,— while before these words were in use, the word nature was used instead. Here, then, if you will consider the matter without stubbornness, we see that evil is that which falls away from essence and tends to nonexistence. *On the Morals of the Manichaeans* 2.2.

B. *Evil has no positive nature.*

603. This Light lighteth also every pure angel, that he may be light not in himself, but in God; from whom if an angel turn away, he becomes impure, as are all those who are called unclean spirits, and are no longer light in the Lord, but darkness in themselves, being deprived of the participation of Light eternal. For evil has no positive nature; but the loss of good has received the name "evil." *City of God* 11.9.

C. *All created substance is good.*

604. Therefore, as they are, they are good; therefore whatsoever is, is good. That evil, then, which I sought whence it was, is not any substance; for were it a substance, it would be good. For either it would be an incorruptible substance, and so a chief good, or a corruptible substance, which unless it were good it could not be corrupted. I perceived, therefore, and it was made clear to me, that Thou didst make all things good, nor is there any substance at all that was not made by Thee; and because all that Thou hast made are not equal, therefore all things are; because individually they are good, and altogether very good, because our God made all things very good. *Confessions* 7.12.

V. Evil is a corruption of substance.

A. Evil *is defined as "corruption."*

605. I ask a third time, What is evil? Perhaps you will reply, Corruption. Undeniably this is a general definition of evil; for corruption implies opposition to nature; and also hurt. But corruption exists not by itself, but in some substance which it corrupts; for corruption itself is not a substance. So the thing which it corrupts is not corruption, is not evil; for what is corrupted suffers the loss of integrity and purity. So that which has no purity to lose cannot be corrupted; and what has, is necessarily good by the participation of purity. Again, what is corrupted is perverted; and what is perverted suffers the loss of order, and order is good. To be corrupted, then, does not imply the absence of good; for in corruption it can be deprived of good, which could not be if there was the absence of good. *On the Morals of the Manichaeans* 5.7.

606. When accordingly it is inquired, whence is evil, it must first be inquired, what is evil, which is nothing else than corruption, either of the measure, or the form, or the order, that belong to nature. Nature therefore which has been corrupted, is called evil, for assuredly when incorrupt it is good; but even when corrupt, so far as it is nature it is good, so far as it is corrupted it is evil. *On the Nature of Good* 4.

B. Evil *as corruption is contrary to nature.*

607. For who can doubt that the whole of that which is called evil is nothing else than corruption? Different evils may, indeed, be called by different names; but that which is the evil of all things in which any evil is perceptible is corruption. So the corruption of an educated mind is ignorance; the corruption of a prudent mind is imprudence; the corruption of a just mind, injustice; the corruption of a brave mind, cowardice; the corruption of a calm, peaceful mind, cupidity, fear, sorrow, pride. Again, in a living body, the corruption of health is pain and disease; the corruption of strength is exhaustion; the corruption of rest is toil. Again, in any corporeal thing, the corruption of beauty is ugliness; the corruption of straightness is crookedness; the corruption of order is confusion; the corruption of entireness is disseverance, or fracture, or diminution. But enough has been said to show that corruption does harm only as displacing the natural condition; and so, that corruption is not nature, but against nature. And if corruption is the only evil to be found anywhere, and if corruption is not nature, no nature is evil. *Against the Epistle of Manichaeus* 35.

C. Corruption is the result of sin.

608. For the corruption of the body, which weighs down the soul, is not the cause but the punishment of the first sin; and it was not the corruptible flesh that made the soul sinful, but the sinful soul that made the flesh corruptible. *City of God* 14.3.

609. Wherefore we must say that the first men were indeed so created, that if they had not sinned, they would not have experienced any kind of death; but that, having become sinners, they were so punished with death, that whatsoever sprang from their stock should also be punished with the same death. For nothing else could be born of them than that which they themselves had been. Their nature was deteriorated in proportion to the greatness of the condemnation of their sin, so that what existed as punishment in those who first sinned, became a natural consequence in their children. For man is not produced by man, as he was from the dust. *City of God* 13.3.

D. The source of this sin is the will (see also 618-628).

610. There is, then, no natural efficient cause, or, if I may be allowed the expression, no essential cause, of the evil will, since itself is the origin of evil in mutable spirits, by which the good of their nature is diminished and corrupted; and the will is made evil by nothing else than defection from God,—a defection of which the cause, too, is certainly deficient. *City of God* 12.9.

611. And I know likewise, that the will could not become evil, were it unwilling to become so; and therefore its failings are justly punished, being not necessary, but voluntary. For its defections are not to evil things, but are themselves evil; that is to say, are not towards things that are naturally and in themselves evil, but the defection of the will is evil, because it is contrary to the order of nature, and an abandonment of that which has supreme being for that which has less. *City of God* 12.8.

VI. Evil is not caused by God.

A. *God is incorruptible, therefore He cannot cause corruption.*

612. In this way, though corruption is an evil, and though it comes not from the Author of natures, but from their being made out of nothing, still, in God's government and control over all that He has made, even corruption is so ordered that it hurts only the lowest natures, for the punishment of the condemned, and for the trial and instruction of the returning, that they may keep near to the incorruptible God, and remain incorrupt, which is our only good; as is said by the prophet, "But it is good for me that I keep near to God." And you must not say, God did not make corruptible natures: for, as far as they are natures, God made them; but as far as they are corruptible, God did not make them: for corruption cannot come from Him who alone is incorruptible. *Against the Epistle of Manichaeus* 38.

B. *God did not cause the first evil will.*

613. But perhaps you are going to ask what is the cause of the movement of the will when it turns from the immutable to the mutable good. That movement is certainly evil, although free will must be numbered among good things since without it no one can live aright. We cannot doubt that that movement of the will, that turning away from the Lord God, is sin; but surely we cannot say that God is the author of sin? God, then, will not be the cause of that movement. *On Free Will* 2.54.

C. God cannot be the cause of evil.

614. Accordingly, when the Catholic Church declares that God is the author of all natures and substances, those who understand this understand at the same time that God is not the author of evil. For how can He who is the cause of the being of all things be at the same time the cause of their not being,—that is, of their falling off from essence and tending to non-existence? For this is what reason plainly declares to be the definition of evil. *On the Morals of the Manichaeans* 2.3.

D. God is not to be blamed for the creature's faults.

615. And this being so, God, who supremely is, and who therefore created every being which has not supreme existence (for that which was made of nothing could not be equal to Him, and indeed could not be at all had He not made it), is not to be found fault with on account of the creature's faults, but is to be praised in view of the natures He has made. *City of God* 12.5.

E. God permits evil so that we desire the future blessed life.

616. Even baptized infants, who are certainly unsurpassed in innocence, are sometimes so tormented, that God, who permits it, teaches us hereby to bewail the calamities of this life, and to desire the felicity of the life to come. As to bodily diseases, they are so numerous that they cannot all be contained even in medical books. And in very many, or almost all of them, the cures and remedies are themselves tortures, so that men are delivered from a pain that destroys by a cure that pains. *City of God* 22.22.

617. How great shall be that felicity, which shall be tainted with no evil, which shall lack no good, and which shall afford leisure for the praises of God, who shall be all in all! For I know not what other employment there can be where no lassitude shall slacken activity, nor any want stimulate to labor. *City of God* 22.30.

VII. The abuse of freedom is the cause of evil (see also chapter 7, Free Will).

A. Evil came through freedom (see 473–500).

618. If the defect we call sin overtook a man against his will, like a fever, the penalty which follows the sinner and is called condemnation would rightly seem to be unjust. But in fact sin is so much a voluntary evil that it is not sin at all unless it is voluntary. This is so obvious that no one denies it, either of the handful of the learned or of the mass of the unlearned. We must either say that no sin has been committed or confess that it has been willingly committed. *Of True Religion* 14. TR

619. But it does not follow that other creatures in the universe are better off merely because they are incapable of misery. That would be like saying that other members of the body are better than the eyes because they can never become blind. A sentient nature even in pain is better than a stone that cannot suffer. In the same way, a rational nature even in misery is higher than one which, because it lacks reason or sensation, cannot suffer misery. *City of God* 12.1.

620. Because if we should again ask wherefore though unwilling he does this, he will say that he is compelled. For every one also who does a thing unwillingly is compelled, and every one who is compelled, if he does a thing, does it only unwillingly. It follows that he that is willing is free from compulsion, even if any one thinks himself compelled. And in this manner every one who willingly does a thing is not compelled, and whoever is not compelled, either does it willingly or not at all. *Two Souls, Against the Manichaeans* 10.14.

B. Evil is freely turning from the infinite good to the lesser good (see 601).

621. Therefore, as I have said, sin is not the striving after an evil nature, but the desertion of a better, and so the deed itself is evil, not the nature which the sinner uses amiss. For it is evil to use amiss that which is good. Whence the apostle reproves certain ones as condemned by divine judgment, "Who have worshipped and served the creature more than the Creator." He does not reprove the creature, which he who should do would act injuriously towards the Creator, but those who, deserting the better, have used amiss the good. *On the Nature of Good* 34.

622. Likewise because sin, or unrighteousness, is not the striving after evil nature but the desertion of better, it is thus found written in the Scriptures: "Every creature of God is good." And accordingly every tree also which God planted in Paradise is assuredly good. Man did not therefore strive after an evil nature when he touched the forbidden tree; but by deserting what was better, he committed an evil deed. Since the Creator is better than any creature which He has made, His command should not have been deserted, that the thing forbidden, however good, might be touched; since the better having been deserted, the good of the creature was striven for, which was touched contrary to the command of the Creator. God did not plant an evil tree in Paradise; but He Himself was better who prohibited its being touched. *On the Nature of Good* 34.

623. However, what is really involved in God's prohibition is obedience, the virtue which is, so to speak, the mother and guardian of all the virtues of a rational creature. The fact is that a rational creature is so constituted that submission is good for it while yielding to its own rather than its Creator's will is, on the contrary, disastrous. *City of God* 14.12.

624. For, when the will, abandoning what is above it, turns itself to something lower, it becomes evil because the very turning itself and not the thing to which it turns is evil. Therefore, an inferior being does not make the will evil but the will itself, because it is a created will, wickedly and inordinately seeks the inferior being. Take the case of two men whose physical and mental make-up is exactly the same. They are both attracted by the exterior beauty of the same person. While gazing at this loveliness, the will of one man is moved with an illicit desire; the will of the other remains firm in its purity. Why did the will become evil in one case and not in the other? What produced the evil will in the man in whom it began to be evil? The physical beauty of the person could not have been the cause, since that was seen by both in exactly the same way and yet both wills did not become evil. Was the cause the flesh of one of those who looked? Then why not the flesh of the other, also? Or was the cause the mind

of one of them? Again, why not the mind of both? For the supposition
is that both are equally constituted in mind and body. *City of God*
12.6.

C. Pride is the beginning of evil.

625. Actually, their bad deed could not have been done had not bad
will preceded it; what is more, the root of their bad will was nothing
else than pride. For, "pride is the beginning of all sin." *City of God*
14.13.

D. Man's misuse of freedom is possible due to his being made out of nothing.

626. Now, the person who talks of a man making his own will evil
must ask why the man made his will evil, whether because he is a
nature or because he is nature made out of nothing? He will learn
that the evil arises not from the fact that the man is a nature, but
from the fact that the nature was made out of nothing. For, if a
nature is the cause of an evil will, then we are compelled to say that
evil springs from good and that good is the cause of evil—since a
bad will comes from a good nature. But how can it come about that
a good, though mutable, nature, even before its will is evil, can
produce something evil, namely, this evil will itself? *City of God* 12.6.

E. All men are affected by the first parents' turn from good (see 373–385).

627. The sin which they committed was so great that it impaired all
human nature—in this sense, that the nature has been transmitted
to posterity with a propensity to sin and a necessity to die. *City of
God* 24.1.

628. Someone may be puzzled by the fact that other sins do not
change human nature in the way that the transgression of our first
parents not merely damaged theirs but had the consequence that
human nature, ever since, has been subject to death. *City of God*
14.12.

VIII. Evil never completely corrupts good.

A. *Every damaged nature was originally good.*

629. The conclusion is that, although no defect can damage an unchangeable good, no nature can be damaged by a defect unless that nature itself is good—for the simple reason that a defect exists only where harm is done. To put the matter in another way: a defect can never be found in the highest good, nor ever apart from some kind of good. *City of God* 12.3.

630. And though it comes not from the Author of natures, but from their being made out of nothing, still, in God's government, and control over all that He has made, even corruption is so ordered that it hurts only the lowest natures, for the punishment of the condemned, and for the trial and instruction of the returning, that they may keep near to the incorruptible God, and remain incorrupt, which is our only good. . . . For, as far as they are natures, God made them; as far as they are corruptible, God did not make them: for corruption cannot come from Him who alone is incorruptible. . . . For in the expression "corruptible nature" there are two words, and not one only. So, in the expression, God made out of nothing, "God" and "nothing" are two separate words. Render therefore to each of these words that which belongs to each, so that the word "nature" may go with the word "God," and the word "corruptible" with the word "nothing." *Against the Epistle of Manichaeus* 38.

B. *Evil is defect in created good.*

631. God is immutable and completely invulnerable. Hence, the malice by which His so-called enemies oppose God is not a menace to Him, but merely bad for themselves—an evil because what is good in their nature is wounded. It is not their nature, but the wound in their nature, that is opposed to God—as evil is opposed to good. *City of God* 12.3.

C. *Evil is never total.*

632. Yet, man did not so fall away from Being as to be absolutely nothing, but, in so far as he turned himself toward himself, he became less than he was when he was adhering to Him who is supreme Being. Thus, no longer to be in God but to be in oneself in the sense of to please oneself is not to be wholly nothing but to be approaching nothingness. *City of God* 14.13.

IX. Evil is part of a total picture of good.

A. *God foresaw but permitted evil.*

633. God was not unaware that man would sin and, being subjected to death, would propagate mortals destined to die; and that these mortals would go so far in the monstrousness of sin that even the beasts without power of rational choice, that had been created in numbers from the waters and the earth, would live more securely and peacefully among their own kind than men—even though the human race had been given a single progenitor for the very purpose of promoting harmony. And, in fact, neither lions nor dragons have ever waged such wars with their own kind as men have fought with one another. However, God also foresaw that a community of saints would be called to supernatural adoption, would have their sins forgiven, be sanctified by the Holy Spirit, and finally be united with the holy angels in eternal peace, so that, at last, the enemy death will be destroyed. And God knew how good it would be for this community often to recall that the human race had its roots in one man, precisely to show how pleasing it is to God that men, though many, should be one. *City of God* 12.22.

634. Here, too, God foresaw the fall, the disregard of His law, the desertion from Good, yet He left man's free choice unchecked because He also foresaw to what good He would turn man's evil. And, in fact, out of this mortal race of men, justly doomed by their own deserts, God gathers, by His grace, so numerous a people that out of them He fills the places and restores the ranks emptied by the fallen angels. Thus is it that the beloved City, which is above, is not deprived of the full complement of its citizens and, in fact, may even rejoice in a fuller complement than it had before the angels' fall. *City of God* 22.1.

B. *It was good for God to permit evil.*

635. Nor can we doubt that God does well even in the permission of what is evil. For He permits it only in the justice of His judgment. And surely all that is just is good. Although, therefore, evil, in so far as it is evil, is not a good; yet the fact that evil as well as good exists, is a good. For if it were not a good that evil should exist, its existence would not be permitted by the omnipotent Good, who without doubt can as easily refuse to permit what He does not wish, as bring about what He does wish. And if we do not believe this, the very first sentence of our creed is endangered, wherein we profess to believe in God the Father Almighty. For He is not truly called Almighty if He cannot do whatsoever He pleases, or if the power of His almighty will is hindered by the will of any creature whatsoever. *Enchiridion* 96.

636. Although, therefore, evil, in so far as it is evil, is not a good; yet the fact that evil as well as good exists, is a good. For if it were not a good that evil should exist, its existence would not be permitted by the omnipotent God, who without doubt can as easily refuse to permit what He does not wish, as bring about what He does wish. *Enchiridion* 96.

C. *God accomplishes a greater good by permitting evil.*

637. Nevertheless, certain heretics remain unconvinced, on the ground that many things in creation are unsuitable and even harmful to that poor and fragile mortality of the flesh which, of course, is no more than the just penalty of sin. The heretics mention, for example, fire, cold, wild beasts, and things like that, without considering how wonderful such things are in themselves and in their proper place and how beautifully they fit into the total pattern of the universe making, as it were, their particular contributions to the commonweal of cosmic beauty. Nor have they observed how valuable they are even to us if only we use them well and wisely. Consider, for instance, poison. It is deadly when improperly used, but when properly applied it turns out to be a health-giving medicine, while, on the contrary, some of those things we like, such as food, drink, and sunlight, when immoderately and unwisely used are seen to be harmful. Thus does Divine Providence teach us not to be foolish in finding fault with things, but, rather, to be diligent in finding out their usefulness or, if our mind and will should fail us in the search, then to believe that there is some hidden use still to be discovered, as in so many other cases, only with great difficulty. *City of God* 11.22.

638. Hence we have an answer to the problem why God should have created men whom He foresaw would sin. It was because both in them and by means of them He could reveal how much was deserved by their guilt and condoned by His grace, and, also, because the harmony of the whole of reality which God has created and controls cannot be marred by the perverse discordancy of those who sin. *City of God* 14.1.

639. For God accomplishes some of His purposes, which of course are all good, through the evil desires of wicked men: for example, it was through the wicked designs of the Jews, working out the good purpose of the Father, that Christ was slain; and this event was so truly good, that when the Apostle Peter expressed his unwillingness that it should take place, he was designated Satan by Him who had come to be slain. *Enchiridion* 101.

640. For as far as relates to their own consciousness, these creatures did what God wished not to be done: but in view of God's omnipotence, they could in no wise effect their purpose. For in the very fact that they acted in opposition to His will, His will concerning them was fulfilled. And hence it is that "the works of the Lord are great, sought out according to all His pleasure," because in a way unspeakably strange and wonderful, even what is done in opposition to His will does not defeat His will. For it would not be done did He not permit it (and of course His permission is not unwilling, but willing); nor would a Good Being permit evil to be done only that in His omnipotence He can turn evil into good. *Enchiridion* 100.

641. For He judged it better to bring good out of evil, than not to permit any evil to exist. And if He had determined that in the case of men, as in the case of the fallen angels, there should be no restoration to happiness, would it not have been quite just, that the being who rebelled against God, who in the abuse of his freedom spurned and transgressed the command of his Creator when he could so easily have kept it, who defaced in himself the image of his Creator by stubbornly turning away from His light, who by an evil use of his free-will broke away from his wholesome bondage to the Creator's laws,—would it not have been just that such a being should have been wholly and to all eternity deserted by God, and left to suffer the everlasting punishment he had so richly earned? Certainly so God would have done, had He been only just and not also merciful, and had He not designed that His unmerited mercy should shine forth the more brightly in contrast with the unworthiness of its objects. *Enchiridion* 27.

9

Ethics

I. The love ethic

A. Supreme love

642. The supreme human law is love and this law is best respected when men, who both desire and ought to live in harmony, so bind themselves by the bonds of social relationships that no man monopolizes more than one relationship, and many different relationships are distributed as widely as possible, so that a common social life of the greatest number may best be fostered. *City of God* 15.16.

643. Therefore hold fast love, and set your minds at rest. Why fearest thou lest thou do evil to some man? Who does evil to the man he loves? Love thou: it is impossible to do this without doing good. *On the Epistle of John* 10.7.

B. The love of God

644. It is a perversion for people to want to enjoy money, but merely to make use of God. Such people do not spend money for the sake of God, but worship God for the sake of money. *City of God* 11.25.

645. Wherefore if you ought not to love even yourself for your own sake, but for Him in whom your love finds its most worthy object, no other man has a right to be angry if you love him too for God's sake.

For this is the law of love that has been laid down by Divine authority. "Thou shalt love thy neighbor as thyself," but, "Thou shalt love
God with all thy heart, and with all thy soul, and with all thy mind:"
so that you are to concentrate all your thoughts, your whole life, and
your whole intelligence upon Him from whom you derive all that
you bring. *On Christian Doctrine* 1.22.

646. As, then, there are four kinds of things that are to be loved,—
first, that which is above us; second, ourselves; third, that which is
on a level with us; fourth, that which is beneath us,—no precepts
need be given about the second and fourth of these. For, however far
a man may fall away from the truth, he still continues to love himself,
and to love his own body. The soul which flies away from the
unchangeable Light, the Ruler of all things, does so that it may rule
over itself and over its own body; and so it cannot but love both itself
and its own body. *On Christian Doctrine* 1.23.

C. The love of self

1. Good self-love

647. Man, therefore, ought to be taught the due measure of loving,
that is, in what measure he may love himself so as to be of service to
himself. For that he does love himself, and does desire to do good to
himself, nobody but a fool would doubt. He is to be taught, too, in
what measure to love his body, so as to care for it wisely and within
due limits. For it is equally manifest that he loves his body also, and
desires to keep it safe and sound. *On Christian Doctrine* 1.25.

648. For though, when the love of God comes first, and the measure
of our love for Him is prescribed in such terms that it is evident all
other things are to find their centre in Him, nothing seems to be said
about our love for ourselves; yet when it is said, "Thou shalt love thy
neighbor as thyself," it at once becomes evident that our love for
ourselves has not been overlooked. *On Christian Doctrine* 1.26.

649. Whoever loves another as himself ought to love that in him
which is his real self. . . . Whoever, then, loves in his neighbor
anything but his real self does not love him as himself. *Of True
Religion* 46. TR

2. Bad self-love

650. What we see, then, is that two societies have issued from two kinds of love. Worldly society has flowered from a selfish love which dared to despise even God, whereas the communion of saints is rooted in a love of God that is ready to trample on self. In a word, this latter relies on the Lord, whereas the other boasts that it can get along by itself. *City of God* 14.28.

651. In fact, this is the main difference which distinguishes the two cities of which we are speaking. The humble City is the society of holy men and good angels; the proud city is the society of wicked men and evil angels. The one City began with the love of God; the other had its beginnings in the love of self. *City of God* 14.13.

652. He ought not to love even himself if he is foolish; for he who loves himself when he is foolish will make no progress toward wisdom. No one will become what he deserves to be unless he hates himself as he is. *Of True Religion* 48. TR

D. Love and virtues

1. Virtue defined

653. As to virtue leading us to a happy life, I hold virtue to be nothing else than perfect love of God. For the fourfold division of virtue I regard as taken from four forms of love. For these four virtues (would that all felt their influence in their minds as they have their names in their mouths!), I should have no hesitation in defining them: that temperance is love giving itself entirely to that which is loved; fortitude is love readily bearing all things for the sake of the loved object; justice is love serving only the loved object, and therefore ruling rightly; prudence is love distinguishing with sagacity between what hinders it and what helps it. The object of this love is not anything, but only God, the chief good, the highest wisdom, the perfect harmony. So we may express the definition thus: that temperance is love keeping itself entire and incorrupt for God; justice is love serving God only, and therefore ruling well all else, as subject to man; prudence is love making a right distinction between what helps it towards God and what might hinder it. *On the Morals of the Catholic Church* 15.

654. I need say no more about right conduct. For if God is man's chief good, which you cannot deny, it clearly follows, since to seek the chief good is to live well, that to live well is nothing else but to love God with all the heart, with all the soul, with all the mind; and, as arising from this, that this love must be preserved entire and incorrupt, which is the part of temperance; that it give way before no troubles, which is the part of fortitude; that it serve no other, which is the part of justice; that it be watchful in its inspection of things lest craft or fraud steal in, which is the part of prudence. This is the one perfection of man, by which alone he can succeed in attaining to the purity of truth. *On the Morals of the Catholic Church* 25.

655. So that it seems to me that it is a brief but true definition of virtue to say, it is the order of love. *City of God* 15.22.

656. When the miser prefers his gold to justice, it is through no fault of the gold, but of the man; and so with every created thing. For though it be good, it may be loved with an evil as well as with a good love: it is loved rightly when it is ordinately; evil, when inordinately. *City of God* 15.22.

2. Virtue discussed

657. The lover, then, whom we are describing, will get from justice this rule of life, that he must with perfect readiness serve the God whom he loves, the highest peace; and as regards all other things, must either rule them as subject to himself, or treat them with a view to their subjection. *On the Morals of the Catholic Church* 24.

a) Prudence

658. With equal brevity we must treat of prudence, to which it belongs to discern between what is to be desired and what is to be shunned. Without this, nothing can be done of what we have already spoken of. It is the part of prudence to keep watch with most anxious vigilance, lest any evil influence should stealthily creep in upon us. Thus the Lord often exclaims, "Watch;" and He says, "Walk while ye have the light, lest darkness come upon you." And then it is said, "Know ye not that a little leaven leaveneth the whole lump?" *On the Morals of the Catholic Church* 24.

b) Fortitude

659. On fortitude we must be brief. The love, then, of which we speak, which ought with all sanctity to burn in desire for God, is called temperance, in not seeking for earthly things, and fortitude, in bearing the loss of them. *On the Morals of the Catholic Church* 22.

660. Then there is the great struggle with pain. But there is nothing, though of iron hardness, which the fire of love cannot subdue. And when the mind is carried up to God in this love, it will soar above all torture free and glorious, with wings beauteous and unhurt, on which chaste love rises to the embrace of God. Otherwise God must allow the lovers of gold, the lovers of praise, the lovers of women, to have more fortitude than the lovers of Himself, though love in those cases is rather to be called passion or lust. And yet even here we may see with what force the mind presses on with unflagging energy, in spite of all alarms, towards that it loves; and we learn that we should bear all things rather than forsake God, since those men bear so much in order to forsake Him. *On the Morals of the Catholic Church* 22.

c) Temperance

661. First, then, let us consider temperance, which promises us a kind of integrity and incorruption in the love by which we are united to God. The office of temperance is in restraining and quieting the passions which make us pant for those things which turn us away from the laws of God and from the enjoyment of His goodness, that is, in a word, from the happy life. *On the Morals of the Catholic Church* 19.

662. The whole duty of temperance, then, is to put off the old man, and to be renewed in God,—that is, to scorn all bodily delights, and the popular applause, and to turn the whole love to things divine and unseen. *On the Morals of the Catholic Church* 19.

E. Virtue and Christianity

663. For though the soul may seem to rule the body admirably, and the reason the vices, if the soul and reason do not themselves obey

God, as God has commanded them to serve Him, they have no proper authority over the body and the vices. For what kind of mistress of the body and the vices can the mind be which is ignorant of the true God? . . . It is for this reason that the virtues [of the natural man] . . . are rather vices than virtues so long as there is no reference to God in the matter. *City of God* 19.25.

F. Virtue, a precondition of truth

664. And as regards the mind, his endeavors are in this order, that he should first fear and then love God. This is true excellence of conduct, and thus the knowledge of the truth is acquired which we are ever in the pursuit of. *On the Morals of the Catholic Church* 28.

665. There is, therefore, something in humility which, strangely enough, exalts the heart, and something in pride which debases it. This seems, indeed, to be contradictory, that loftiness should debase and lowliness exalt. But pious humility enables us to submit to what is above us; and nothing is more exalted above us than God; and therefore humility, by making us subject to God, exalts us. *City of God* 14.13.

II. Ethical dilemmas

A. General conflicts

1. Determination by God of the greater sin

666. What sins are trivial and what are grand, however, is not for human but for divine judgment to determine. *Enchiridion* 78.

667. Again, there are some sins which would be considered very trifling, if the Scriptures did not show that they are really very serious. For who would suppose that the man who says to his brother, "Thou fool," is in danger of hell-fire, did not He who is the Truth say so? *Enchiridion* 79.

2. Greater obligations of love

668. Now he is a man of just and holy life who forms an unprejudiced estimate of things, and keeps his affections also under strict control, so that he neither loves what he ought not to love, nor fails to love what he ought to love, nor loves that more which ought to be loved less, nor loves that equally which ought to be loved either less or more, nor loves that less or more which ought to be loved equally. *On Christian Doctrine* 1.28.

3. Equal love for all men and special regard
   for the immediate

669. Further, all men are to be loved equally. But since you cannot do good to all, you are to pay special regard to those who, by the accidents of time, or place, or circumstance, are brought into closer connection with you. For, suppose that you had a great deal of some commodity, and felt bound to give it away to somebody who had none, and that it could not be given to more than one person; if two persons presented themselves, neither of whom had either from need or relationship a greater claim upon you than the other, you could do nothing fairer than choose by lot to which you would give what could not be given to both. Just so among men: since you cannot consult for the good of them all, you must take the matter as decided for you by a sort of lot, according as each man happens for the time being to be more closely connected with you. *On Christian Doctrine* 1.28.

B. Special cases

670. The same divine law which forbids the killing of a human being allows certain exceptions, as when God authorizes killing by a general law [just war] or when He gives an explicit commission to an individual for a limited time.

1. General—the waging of war
2. Special—Abraham, Jephthah, Samson

City of God 1.21.

671. But, they say, in the time of persecution some holy women escaped those who menaced them with outrage, by casting themselves into rivers which they knew would drown them; and having died in this manner, they are venerated in the church catholic as martyrs. Of such persons I do not presume to speak rashly. I cannot tell whether there may not have been vouchsafed to the church some divine authority, proved by trustworthy evidences, for so honoring their memory: it may be that it is so. It may be they were not deceived by human judgment, but prompted by divine wisdom, to their act of self-destruction. We know that this was the case with Samson. And when God enjoins any act, and intimates by plain evidence that He has enjoined it, who will call obedience criminal? Who will accuse so religious a submission? But then every man is not justified in sacrificing his son to God, because Abraham was commendable in so doing. The soldier who has slain a man in obedience to the authority under which he is lawfully commissioned, is not accused of murder by any law of his state; nay, if he has not slain him, it is then he is accused of treason to the state, and of despising the law. But if he has been acting on his own authority, and at his own impulse, he has in this case incurred the crime of shedding human blood. *City of God* 1.26.

672. But this we affirm, this we maintain, this we every way pronounce to be right, that no man ought to inflict on himself voluntary death, for this is to escape the ills of time by plunging into those of eternity; that no man ought to do so on account of another man's sins, for this were to escape a guilt which could not pollute him, by incurring great guilt of his own; that no man ought to do so on account of his own past sins, for he has all the more need of this life that these sins may be healed by repentance; that no man should put an end to this life to obtain that better life we look for after death, for those who die by their own hand have no better life after death. *City of God* 1.26

III. Specific ethical issues

A. War

673. For it is the wrong-doing of the opposing party which compels the wise man to wage just wars; and this wrong-doing even though it gives rise to no war, would still be matter of grief to man because it is man's wrong-doing. *City of God* 19.7.

674. It is therefore with the desire for peace that wars are waged. . . . And hence it is obvious that peace is the end sought by war. For every man seeks peace by waging war, but no man seeks war by waging peace. *City of God* 19.7.

675. But if the house of David could not earn peace on any other terms except that Absalom his son should have been slain in the war which he was waging against his father, although he had most carefully given strict injunctions to his followers that they should use their utmost endeavors to preserve him alive and safe, that his paternal affection might be able to pardon him on his repentance, what remained for him except to weep for the son that he had lost, and to console himself in his sorrow by reflecting on the acquisition of peace for his kingdom? The same, then, is the case with the Catholic Church, our mother; for when war is waged against her by men who are certainly different from sons, since it must be acknowledged that from the great tree, which by the spreading of its branches is extended over all the world, this little branch in Africa is broken off, whilst she is willing in her love to give them birth, that they may return to the root, without which they cannot have the true life, at the same time if she collects the remainder in so large a number by the loss of some, she soothes and cures the sorrow of her maternal heart by the thoughts of the deliverance of such mighty nations; especially when she considers that those who are lost perish by a death which they brought upon themselves, and not, like Absalom, by the fortune of war. *Correction of the Donatists* 8.32.

B. Suicide

676. It is not without significance, that in no passage of the holy canonical books there can be found either divine precept or permission to take away our own life, whether for the sake of entering on the enjoyment of immortality, or of shunning, or ridding ourselves of anything whatever. Nay, the law, rightly interpreted, even prohibits suicide, where it says, "Thou shalt not kill." This is proved especially by the omission of the words "thy neighbor," which are inserted when false witness is forbidden: "Thou shalt not bear false witness against thy neighbor." *City of God* 1.20.

677. Yet, they overcame the word, not by defending themselves, but by preferring to die for Christ. *City of God* 22.9.

C. Lying

1. Piously intended falsehoods are wrong.

678. For if the Apostle Paul did not speak the truth when, finding fault with the Apostle Peter, he said: "If thou, being a Jew, livest after the manner of Gentiles, and not as do the Jews, why compellest thou the Gentiles to live as do the Jews?"—if, indeed, Peter seemed to him to be doing what was right, and if, notwithstanding, he, in order to soothe troublesome opponents, both said and wrote that Peter did what was wrong;—if we say thus, what then shall be our answer when perverse men such as he himself prophetically described arise, forbidding marriage, if they defend themselves by saying that, in all which the same apostle wrote in confirmation of the lawfulness of marriage, he was, on account of men who, through love for their wives, might become troublesome opponents, declaring what was false,—saying these things, forsooth, not because he believed them, but because their opposition might thus be averted? It is unnecessary to quote many parallel examples. For even things which pertain to the praises of God might be represented as piously intended falsehoods, written in order that love for Him might be enkindled in men who were slow of heart; and thus nowhere in the sacred books shall the authority of pure truth stand sure. *Letters* 28.34.

2. It is never right to lie, even to save a life.

679. How much braver then, how much more excellent, to say, "I will neither betray nor lie?"

This did a former Bishop of the Church of Thagasta, Firmus by name, and even more firm in will. For, when he was asked by command of the emperor, through officers sent by him, for a man who was taking refuge with him, and whom he kept in hiding with all possible care, he made answer to their questions, that he could neither tell a lie, nor betray a man; and when he had suffered so many torments of body, (for as yet emperors were not Christian,) he stood firm in his purpose. Thereupon being brought before the emperor, his conduct appeared so admirable, that he without any difficulty obtained a pardon for the man whom he was trying to save. What conduct could be more brave and constant? *On Lying* 22,23.

3. Apparent lies can be explained.

680. The explanation is found in this, that he took part in the Jewish sacrifices, as being himself by birth a Jew; and that when he said all this which I have quoted, he meant, not that he pretended to be what he was not, but that he felt with true compassion that he must bring such help to them as would be needful for himself if he were involved in their error. *Letters* 40.4.

4. One falsehood undermines the whole Bible.

681. Manifestly, therefore, Peter was truly corrected, and Paul has given a true narrative of the event, unless, by the admission of a falsehood here, the authority of the Holy Scriptures given for the faith of all coming generations is to be made wholly uncertain and wavering. For it is neither possible nor suitable to state within the compass of a letter how great and how unutterably evil must be the consequences of such a concession. *Letters* 40.4.

5. Every sin is a lie.

682. When a man lives "according to man" and not "according to God" he is like the Devil. . . . Wherefore it is not without meaning said that all sin is a lie. For no sin is committed save by that desire or will by which we desire that it be well with us, and shrink from it being ill with us. That, therefore, is a lie which we do in order that it may be well with us, but which makes us more miserable than we were. *City of God* 14.4.

D. Rape

683. I affirm, therefore, that in case of violent rape and of an unshaken intention not to yield unchaste consent, the crime is attributed only to the ravisher and not at all to the ravished. *City of God* 1.19.

E. Sex

1. Sex, even in marriage, can be shameful.

684. Such, however, is the present condition of mortal men, that the connubial intercourse and lust are at the same time in action; and on this account it happens, that as the lust is blamed, so also the nuptial commerce, however lawful and honourable, is thought to be reprehensible by those persons who either are unwilling or unable to draw the distinction between them. *On Original Sin* 42.

2. Sex for pleasure, even in marriage, is sinful.

685. But in the married, as these things are desirable and praiseworthy, so the others are to be tolerated, that no lapse occur into damnable sins; that is, into fornications and adulteries. To escape this evil, even such embraces of husband and wife as have not procreation for their object, but serve as overbearing concupiscence, are permitted, so far as to be within range of forgiveness, though not prescribed by way of commandment: and the married pair are enjoined not to defraud one the other, lest Satan should tempt them by reason of their incontinence. *On Marriage and Concupiscence* 1.16.

3. Polygamy for propagation is better than monogamy for pleasure.

686. For, if it was possible for one man to use many wives with chastity, it is possible for another to use one wife with lust. And I look with greater approval on the man who uses the fruitfulness of many wives for the sake of an ulterior object, than on the man who enjoys the body of one wife for its own sake. For in the former case the man aims at a useful object suited to the circumstances of the times; in the latter case he gratifies a lust which is engrossed in temporal enjoyments. And those men to whom the apostle permitted as a matter of indulgence to have one wife because of their incontinence, were less near to God than those who, though they had each of them numerous wives, yet just as a wise man uses food and drink only for the sake of bodily health, used marriage only for the sake of offspring. And, accordingly, if these last had been still alive at the advent of our Lord, when the time not of casting stones away but of gathering them together had come, they would have immediately made themselves eunuchs for the kingdom of heaven's sake. For there is no difficulty in abstaining unless when there is lust in enjoying. *On Christian Doctrine* 3.18.

F. Nudity

687. Because it is a shamefully wicked thing to strip the body naked at a banquet among the drunken and licentious, it does not follow that it is a sin to be naked in the baths. *On Christian Doctrine* 3.12.

G. Gluttony

688. We must, therefore, consider carefully what is suitable to times and places and persons, and not rashly charge men with sins. For it is possible that a wise man may use the daintiest food without any sin of epicurism or gluttony, while a fool will crave for the vilest food with a most disgusting eagerness of appetite. . . . For in all matters of this kind it is not the nature of the things we use, but our reason for using them, and our manner of seeking them, that make what we do either praiseworthy or blameable. *On Christian Doctrine* 3.12.

H. Ethics and progressive revelation

689. Therefore, although all, or nearly all, the transactions recorded in the Old Testament are to be taken not literally only, but figuratively as well, nevertheless even in the case of those which the reader has taken literally, and which, though the authors of them are praised, are repugnant to the habits of the good men who since our Lord's advent are the custodians of the divine commands, let him refer the figure to its interpretation, but let him not transfer the act to his habits of life. For many things which were done as duties at that time, cannot now be done except through lust. *On Christian Doctrine* 3.22.

I. Polygamy

690. Now the saints of ancient times were, under the form of an earthly kingdom, foreshadowing and foretelling the kingdom of heaven. And on account of the necessity for a numerous offspring, the custom of one man having several wives was at that time blameless: and for the same reason it was not proper for one woman to have several husbands, because a woman does not in that way become more fruitful, but, on the contrary, it is base harlotry to seek either gain or offspring by promiscuous intercourse. In regard to matters of this sort, whatever the holy men of those times did without lust, Scripture passes over without blame, although they did things which could not be done at the present time, except through lust. And everything of this nature that is there narrated we are to take not only in its historical and literal, but also in its figurative and prophetical sense, and to interpret as bearing ultimately upon the end of love towards God or our neighbor, or both. For as it was disgraceful among the ancient Romans to wear tunics reaching to the heels, and furnished with sleeves, but now it is disgraceful for men honorably born not to wear tunics of that description: so we must take heed in regard to other things also, that lust do not mix with our use of them; for lust not only abuses to wicked ends the customs of those among whom we live, but frequently also transgressing the bounds of custom, betrays, in a disgraceful outbreak, its own hideousness, which was concealed under the cover of prevailing fashions. *On Christian Doctrine* 3.12.